Able MUSE

A REVIEW OF POETRY, PROSE & ART

NUMBER 16

Winter 2013

www.ablemuse.com

Now available from Able Muse Press:

Able Muse Anthology
Edited by Alexander Pepple
Foreword by Timothy Steele

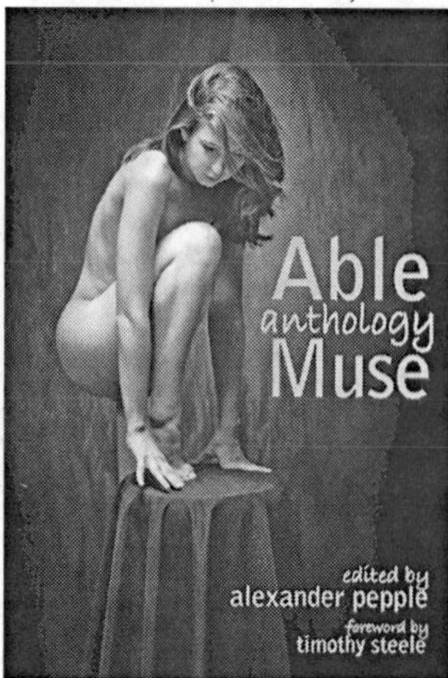

978-0-9865338-0-8 • $16.95

With R.S. Gwynn, Rhina P. Espaillat, Rachel Hadas, Mark Jarman, Timothy Murphy, Dick Davis, A.E. Stallings, Alan Sullivan, Deborah Warren, Diane Thiel, Leslie Monsour, Kevin Durkin, Turner Cassity, Kim Bridgford, Richard Moore and others.

". . . Here's a generous serving of the cream of Able Muse including not only formal verse but nonmetrical work that also displays careful craft, memorable fiction (seven remarkable stories), striking artwork and photography, and incisive prose." — *X.J. Kennedy*

Able Muse - **Inaugural Print Edition**

WITH:

POEMS, FICTION, BOOK REVIEWS, INTERVIEWS & ESSAYS from catherine tufariello • catharine savage brosman • leslie monsour • ned balbo • ted mc carthy • diane seuss • susan mclean • rebecca foust • j. patrick lewis • john slater • gail white • kim bridgford • nancy lou canyon • john whitworth • peter filkins • marilyn l. taylor • and others

ISBN 978-0-9865338-2-2

Subscribe to: *Able Muse (Print Ed.)*

~ **Print Edition** ~

Semiannual review of poetry, prose & art

Able Muse (Print Edition) continues the excellence in poetry, art, fiction, essays, interviews and book reviews we've brought you all these years in the online edition. Subscribe at *www.ablemusepress.com*

For complete details, visit: **www.AbleMusePress.com**

visit

online for more than a decade of archives, plus web-only features not available in the print edition at:

www.ablemuse.com

***Able Muse** is not just another poetry site. It is one of the best sites on the Internet.*
—Heather O'Neil, *Suite101.com*

***Able Muse*'s premier online forums and workshops for metrical and non-metrical poetry, fiction, translations, art, nonfiction and discussions at:**

http://eratosphere.ablemuse.com

***Able Muse** and its extraordinary companion website, the **Eratosphere,** have created a huge and influential virtual literary community.* —Dana Gioia

Able Muse
www.ablemuse.com

Editor	Alexander Pepple
Assistant Poetry Editors	Peter Austin, Reagan Upshaw
Nonfiction Editor	Gregory Dowling
Fiction Editor	Karen Kevorkian
Assistant Fiction Editors	Keith J. Powell, John Riley, Janice D. Soderling, Rob Wright
Editorial Board	Rachel Hadas, X.J. Kennedy, A.E. Stallings, Timothy Steele, Deborah Warren

Able Muse is published semiannually. Subscription rates for individuals: $24.00 per year; libraries and institutions: $34 per year; single and previous issues: $16.95 + $3 S&H.
International subscription rate: $33 per year; single and previous issues: $16.95 + $5 S&H.
Subscribe online at www.ablemusepress.com or send a check payable to *Able Muse Review* to the snail mail address indicated below. (USD throughout. Online payment with PayPal/credit card.)

We read year-round and welcome previously unpublished manuscripts only. No simultaneous submissions. Online or email submissions ONLY. Submission guidelines available at: www.ablemuse.com/submit

Queries and other correspondence should be emailed to: editor@ablemuse.com
For paper correspondence, be sure to include a self-addressed, stamped envelope.

Library of Congress Control Number: 2013920754

ISBN 978-1-927409-27-5 (paperback) / ISBN 978-1-927409-28-2 (digital)

ISSN 2168-0426

Cover image: "The Lonely Heart" by Peter Svensson

Cover & book design by Alexander Pepple

Attn: Alexander Pepple, Editor
Able Muse Review
467 Saratoga Avenue #602
San Jose, CA 95129

www.ablemuse.com
editor@ablemuse.com

Printed in the United States of America
Published in 2013 by Able Muse Press: www.ablemusepress.com

Alexander Pepple

Editorial

This issue proudly presents the winners and finalists of the third annual *Able Muse* contests. Also included are new poems from Jehanne Dubrow, our featured poet, recipient of numerous writing awards. She speaks about her poetic craft and themes in an interview by Anna M. Evans. Our showcased artist Peter Svensson discusses the sources of inspiration for his amazing black-and-white photography.

The youngest poet we've published to date, 14-year-old Alex Greenberg whose writing is seasoned beyond his years, shares our poetry pages with Rachel Hadas, R.S. Gwynn, Catharine Savage Brosman, Richard Wakefield, and Marly Youmans. Chris Childers caps his translations of four charming epithalamia by Sappho, Theocritus and Catullus with a with a like-themed poem of his own.

Congratulations to the top winners and finalists of the 2013 Able Muse Write Prize for Poetry as selected by final judge Kelly Cherry: D.R. Goodman, the winner, for her poem "The Face of Things"; Jeanne Wagner, whose poem "The Unfaithful Shepherd" placed second; and Richard Wakefield, third with "Keepaway."

The proud tradition of the essay is upheld splendidly by A.E. Stallings (on Hecht and Horace), Philip Morre (on Edward Thomas and rain), Peter Byrne (on Tennyson and Lear), and tandem essays from David Mason, and from Chrissy Mason—a conjugal bonanza and possibly a literary first. Don't miss the book review by Rory Waterman of *Deep Field* by Philip Gross, or from Jane Hammons, our first review of a novel—*The Translator* by Nina Schuyler.

Fiction is richly represented with stories from Cheryl Diane Kidder, Blaine Vitallo, Charles Wilkinson, and a feature is "Crown of Iguanas" from Donna Laemmlen, the winner of the 2013 Able Muse Write Prize for fiction, selected by final judge Thaisa Frank.

Congratulations to Melissa Balmain, winner of the 2013 Able Muse Book Award for her manuscript *Walking in on People,* selected by final judge X.J. Kennedy. For the first time in the award's history, our final judge nominated a manuscript worthy of special recognition and publication—the second-place *Cup* by Jeredith Merrin. Some of our finalists will also receive a standard Able Muse Press publication contract. A special thank you to the accomplished poets and writers who participated in our blind reading and shortlisting in the early judging stages.

We have made six nominations for the 2014 Pushcart Prize. These include a poem from the previous issue ("A Miracle for Breakfast" by Jen DeGregorio); four from the current one ("Synecdoche Island" by R.S. Gwynn, "The Nut House" by Tara Tatum, "Requited Love" by Matthew Buckley Smith, and "Keepaway" by Richard Wakefield); and a story from the current issue ("How the West Was Won" by Cheryl Diane Kidder).

We are now open for submissions to the 2014 run of *Able Muse* contests. We are honored to have three illustrious final judges: Dick Allen for the Write Prize for poetry, Amit Majmudar for the Write Prize for fiction; and Molly Peacock for the Able Muse Book Award. Entry deadlines are provided in these pages, and details at the Able Muse Press website, www.ablemusepress.com.

Submissions are open year-round for our regular issues, and still open for the special translation issue next summer, 2014, with acclaimed poet, critic and translator Charles Martin as guest editor. Details are available online at www.ablemuse.com/submit/.

Able Muse Press has been busy with the release of new books of poetry, including the second full-length collections from Maryann Corbett (finalist for the 2011 Able Muse Book Award) and Barbara Ellen Sorensen. We have also released the first full-length collections from the 2012 Able Muse Book Award finalists Carol Light, Ellen Kaufman and Stephen Scaer, and also the winning collection from the 2012 Able Muse Book Award: *Virtue, Big as Sin* by Frank Osen.

I am pleased to introduce our new fiction editor Karen Kevorkian. We are grateful to our departing fiction editor Nina Schuyler for all that she has done for *Able Muse* fiction and wish her much success promoting her new book, *The Translator* (Pegasus, 2013). We welcome our new assistant editors Peter Austin and Reagan Upshaw for poetry, and Keith J. Powell and Rob Wright for fiction. We offer thanks to our departing assistant editors Jonathan Scott for poetry and Tim Love for fiction, as well as to our returning assistant fiction editors Janice D. Soderling and John Riley, and our nonfiction editor Gregory Dowling.

We appreciate your continued support of *Able Muse* and Able Muse Press, and hope you'll enjoy this issue as much as we've enjoyed bringing it to you.

The very best,

Alexander Pepple
—Editor

BOOKS
FROM
ABLE MUSE PRESS

NEW & RECENT RELEASES

FRANK OSEN
Virtue, Big as Sin - Poems
~ WINNER, 2012 **ABLE MUSE BOOK AWARD** ~

BARBARA ELLEN SORENSEN
Compositions of the Dead Playing Flutes - Poems

ELLEN KAUFMAN
House Music - Poems

JAMES POLLOCK
Sailing to Babylon - Poems

MATTHEW BUCKLEY SMITH
Dirge for an Imaginary World - Poems
~ WINNER, 2011 **ABLE MUSE BOOK AWARD** ~

APRIL LINDNER
This Bed Our Bodies Shaped - Poems

JAMES RICHARD WAKEFIELD
A Vertical Mile - Poems

MICHAEL CANTOR
Life in the Second Circle - Poems

AARON POOCHIGIAN
The Cosmic Purr - Poems

HOLLIS SEAMON
Corporeality - Stories

CAROL LIGHT
Heaven from Steam - Poems

STEPHEN SCAER
Pumpkin Chucking - Poems

MARYANN CORBETT
Credo for the Checkout Line in Winter - Poems

WENDY VIDELOCK
The Dark Gnu and Other Poems

BEN BERMAN
Strange Borderlands - Poems

CATHERINE CHANDLER
Lines of Flight - Poems

MARGARET ANN GRIFFITHS
Grasshopper: The Poetry of M A Griffiths

WENDY VIDELOCK
Nevertheless - Poems

2013 SPRING/SUMMER CATALOG

Free Download at: **www.ablemusepress.com/catalog**

A B L E M U S E W R I T E P R I Z E

2014 Able Muse **Write Prize**
for poetry & fiction

» ***$500 prize*** *for the poetry winner*
» *All poetry styles welcome (metrical & free verse)*
»
» ***$500 prize*** *for the fiction winner*

» *plus,* ***publication*** *in Able Muse (Print Edition)*

» ***Blind judging*** *by the final judges*

» ***Final Judges****:* *Dick Allen (poetry);*
Amit Majmudar (fiction)

» ***Entry Deadline:*** *February 15, 2014*

GUIDELINES & ENTRY INFORMATION
AVAILABLE ONLINE AT:

www.ablemusepress.com

ABLE MUSE BOOK PRIZE

2014 Able Muse Book Award
for poetry

- ***$1000 prize*** *for winning manuscript, plus*
- ***publication*** *by Able Muse Press*
- *All poetry styles welcome (metrical & free verse)*
- ***Blind judging*** *by the final judge*
- ***Final Judge**: Molly Peacock*
- ***Entry Deadline:** March 31, 2014*

GUIDELINES & ENTRY INFORMATION AVAILABLE ONLINE AT:

www.ablemusepress.com

Able Muse - Print Edition, No. 14

Winter 2012
With

POETRY, FICTION, BOOK REVIEWS, INTERVIEWS & ESSAYS from nicolas evariste ▪ catherine tufariello ▪ catharine savage brosman ▪ thomas carper ▪ lorna knowles blake ▪ richard wakefield ▪ timothy murphy ▪ kathryn locey ▪ tony barnstone ▪ len krisak ▪ evelyn somers ▪ gigi mark ▪ gregory dowling ▪ michael cohen ▪ peter byrne ▪ aaron poochigian ▪ and others

ISBN 978-1-927409-07-7

~ GET YOUR COPY AT ~

Able Muse Press: www.ablemusepress.com

Or

Amazon Worldwide: www.amazon.com

superstition [review]

an online literary magazine

featuring...

Barbara Hamby
Chase Twichell
Lee Martin
Brenda Hillman
Dinty W. Moore
Kazim Ali
Billy Collins
Kelle Groom
Dan Chaon
Barbara Kingsolver

"So many online magazines start out with great promise and so many go under almost immediately. [SR] is one of the country's real and important successes."

Dick [Allen]

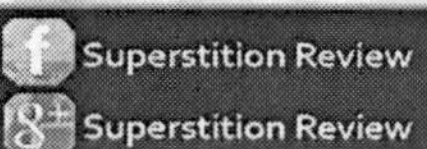

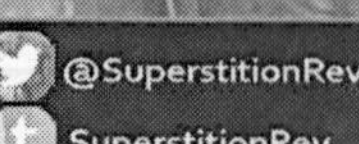

superstition.review@gmail.com superstitionreview.com

Able MUSE

A REVIEW OF POETRY, PROSE & ART

After more than a decade of online publishing excellence, Able Muse began a bold new chapter with its print edition

Check out our 12+ years of online archives for work by

Rachel Hadas • X.J. Kennedy • Timothy Steele • Mark Jarman • A.E. Stallings • Dick Davis • A.M. Juster • Timothy Murphy • Annie Finch • Deborah Warren • Chelsea Rathburn • Rhina P. Espaillat • Turner Cassity • Richard Moore • Stephen Edgar • David Mason • Thaisa Frank • • Nina Schuyler • Solitaire Miles • Misha Gordin • and others

SUBSCRIPTION

Able Muse - Print Edition

Able Muse is published semiannually.

Subscription rates for individuals: $24.00 per year; single and previous issues: $16.95 + $3 S&H.

International subscription rate: $33 per year; single and previous issues: $16.95 + $5 S&H. (USD throughout.)

Subscribe online with PayPal/ credit card at

www.ablemusepress.com

Or send a check payable to *Able Muse Review*

Attn: Alex Pepple - Editor, Able Muse,
467 Saratoga Avenue #602,
San Jose, CA 95129 USA

CONTENTS

FEATURED ARTIST

2013 Write Prize for Poetry:

POETRY

FICTION

2013 WRITE PRIZE FOR FICTION ▪ WINNER

BOOK REVIEWS

Congratulations to the 2013 Able MUSE CONTEST WINNERS

2013 Able Muse Write Prize

Fiction
Final Judge: **Thaisa Frank**

WINNER
Donna Laemmlen
"Crown of Iguanas"

Poetry
Final Judge: **Kelly Chery**

WINNER
D.R. Goodman
"The Face of Things"

SECOND PLACE:
Jeanne Wagner

THIRD PLACE:
Richard Wakefield

FINALISTS
- Melissa Balmain
- Anna M. Evans
- D.R. Goodman
- D.R. Goodman
- Tara Tatum

2013 Able Muse Book Award

Poetry Manuscript
Final Judge: **X.J. Kennedy**

WINNER
Melissa Balmain
Walking in on People

SECOND PLACE
Jeredith Merrin
Cup

FINALISTS
William Conelly
Uncontested Grounds

D. R. Goodman
Greed: A Confession

J.D. Smith
The Killing Tree

Chelsea Woodard
Vellum

Books from some of the finalists also coming soon from Able Muse Press!

HONORABLE MENTION
Lucia Galloway • Elise Hempel • Richard Meyer • Rob Wright

Virtue, Big as Sin

Poems

by Frank Osen

***NEW~ *from* Able Muse Press**

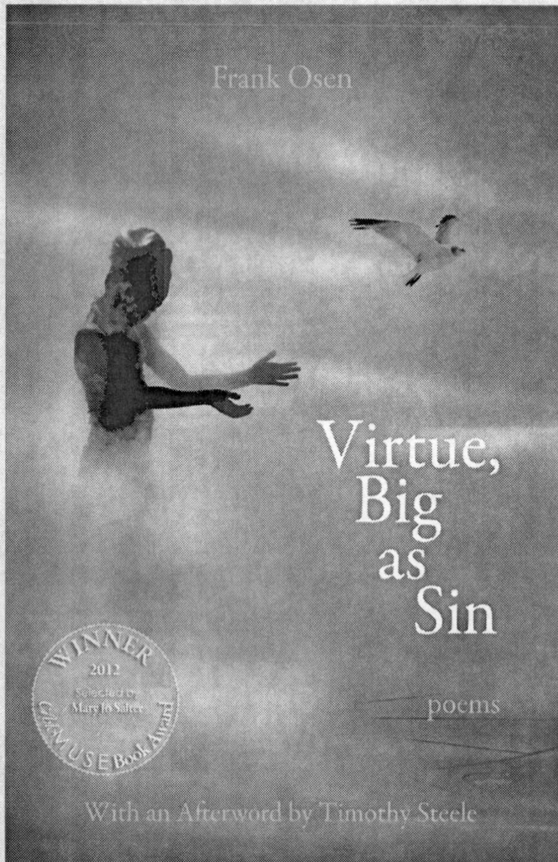

WINNER
2012 Able Muse Book Award

PRAISE FOR *VIRTUE, BIG AS SIN*
(with an Afterword by Timothy Steele)

The first full-length collection from Frank Osen

★★★★★

"Frank Osen's Virtue, Big as Sin *offers one witty, elegant poem after another."*
— Mary Jo Salter (Judge, 2012 Able Muse Book Award)

"A talent for tragedy and comedy, and for mixing them."
— Timothy Steele (from the afterword)

"Virtue, Big as Sin *has left me with the sense of satisfaction and enduring pleasure."*
— Rhina P. Espaillat

"Frank Osen's poems revel in beauty and pleasure, in technical dexterity and high-gloss finish."
— Dick Davis

ISBN 978-1-927409-16-9 / 84 pages

ORDER NOW FROM ABLE MUSE PRESS AT: WWW.ABLEMUSEPRESS.COM
OR, ORDER FROM AMAZON.COM, BN.COM, . . . & OTHER ONLINE OR OFFLINE BOOKSTORES

www.AbleMusePress.com

R.S. Gwynn

Synecdoche Island

— Homage to Roz Chast

Hand's farms are burnt. Foot marches back and forth
While Tongue wags rumors of invading North
And Loin girds up for battle. Old, bent Knee,
(That craven!) holds no hope of victory,
Nor do pale Brow and fluttering Pulse. Still, Nose,
Who knows the news, blows loudly, bracing those
Who waver, spreading zeal on Harry Chest
And Manley Shoulders, and both do their best
To raise Arms and faint Heart to bear the yoke,
Shaming fat Butt, who's once again the joke.
Inclined to making love instead of war,
Poor Richard limps and hangs around the shore,
Sadly casting an undry eye towards home
Across the unplumb'd, salt, estranging foam.

R.S. Gwynn

Looney Tunes

— For John Whitworth

It begins with the division of a solitary cell,
Carcinogenetic fission leading to a passing-bell,
Lurking far beneath your vision like a pebble in a well—
Then it grows.
Soon enough there comes a scalpel that is keen to save your life,
Crooning, "All things will be well, pal, if you just endure the knife,
But to climb the tallest Alp'll be much easier. Call your wife."
Then it grows, grows, grows. Then it grows.

Say you can't remember Monday night when Tuesday rolls around.
Does it mean they'll find you one day blind and frothing on the ground?
Is it ominous that Sunday sermons make your temples pound?
(How it shows!)
You may take the pledge, abstaining, thinking you can lick it all.
But it's hard when, ascertaining how diversions may enthrall,
You're still standing there and draining one well past the final call:
How it shows, shows, shows. (How it shows!)

You may lose a set of car keys and mislay a name or face.
Does your mind demand bright marquees where each star must have its place?
It's like diving in the dark. It's less a river than a race.
            And it flows
Like the coming days of drivel, like the dreaded days of drool
When the very best you'll give'll prove you're just an antique fool,
And your thoughts will be so trivial as to lead to ridicule—
      And it flows, flows, flows. And it flows.

Do you want to be a burden? Can you bear to be a drag?
Make your mind up, say the word and do not let the moment lag.
When you go to get your guerdon let them see your battle flag!
            So it goes.
There'll be many there who'll miss you and a few to lend a hand,
There'll be baskets full of tissue, lots of awful music and
Lissome maidens who won't kiss you as you seek the promised land.
      So it goes, goes, goes. So it goes.

Philip Morre

Reading Edward Thomas's "It Rains" and Other Rain Poems

It Rains

It rains, and nothing stirs within the fence
Anywhere through the orchard's untrodden, dense
Forest of parsley. The great diamonds
Of rain on the grassblades there is none to break,
Or the fallen petals further down to shake.

And I am nearly as happy as possible
To search the wilderness in vain though well,
To think of two walking, kissing there,
Drenched, yet forgetting the kisses of the rain:
Sad, too, to think that never, never again,

Unless alone, so happy shall I walk
In the rain. When I turn away, on its fine stalk
Twilight has fined to naught, the parsley flower
Figures, suspended still and ghostly white,
The past hovering as it revisits the light.

Edward Thomas is something of a special case in English poetry (and who isn't, to his or her pleaders?) in various ways, not all of them, I want to argue, much aired. I fear that, viewed from the United States, he may be hardly a case at all, at best some kind of pilot fish swimming alongside Robert Frost. A recent (American) publication, supposedly listing the *100 Essential Modern Poems* in English, found no space for him at all, while including any number of inferior talents. And yet Ted Hughes, in a speech to mark the placing of a stone to commemorate the First World War poets in Westminster Abbey, called him "the father of us all."

Thomas's first and most obvious claim to specialcaseness is the brevity of his poetic career: he wrote his first poem in December 1914 when he was already 36 and the last, so far as we know, in January 1917, before dying at the Battle of Arras in April—a span that makes Rimbaud look like a careerist. In those hardly more than two years, however, he wrote 142 poems, nearly all included in two books, *Poems* (1917) and *Last Poems* (1918), both posthumous, though the first was seen by him most of the way to, if not through, the press.

Another minor anomaly has to do with Edward Thomas's status as a "war poet." All of his poems were written during the First World War but none of them from the battlefield. He seems, in fact, for whatever reason, to have written nothing more after his arrival in France, early in 1917. On the other hand, several poems ("As the Team's Head-brass" most memorably) deal directly with the effects of the war on the English countryside, and in many others the war is a more or less overt presence in the background.

The poem I have chosen to look at here is perhaps not one of his greatest, though a favorite of mine. It has several obvious faults, for a start: there are two thumping inversions in the first strophe, of which the one in the last line, "the fallen petals further down to shake," is seriously awkward. The "though well" ending the second line of the second strophe does seem a little dragged in for the rhyme, and only a half rhyme at that. Similarly "dense" in line 2, though actually quite justified as to sense, because of its positioning is so thrust at us as to seem forced. Some have objected to the rather fraught syntax of the closing four-line sentence, but as long as you're not tempted to pause after "stalk," it seems to me to work well enough. One of my reasons too for choosing a less than perfect piece is to remind us that Edward Thomas was really a beginner all his poetic life, not that he reads like it, most of the time. Which of us wouldn't blush at some of the things we wrote less than eighteen months from starting out?

Also, I mean to cheat a little by including the whole of another—his grandest—rain poem at the end. But to return to the poem in hand, it has been noted by more than one commentator that happiness for Thomas is nearly always recalled, or rather, lies in the recalling. This is expressed with peculiar force and poignancy here with the very canny (for a tyro!) device of splitting "never, never again" from the unexpected "unless alone" over a verse break. He has much higher expectations of happiness walking wetly alone in the orchard, remembering, than walking there with any companion past or yet to be met or imagined. You may want to say at this point: "Hang on a moment. Surely you mean 'the speaker,' rather than ET?" But in fact it is a characteristic of Thomas's poetry that "I" is always, or nearly always, himself. This is most obvious in the lovely sequence of testamentary poems to his children:

If I should ever by chance grow rich
I'll buy Codham, Cockridden and Childerditch,
Roses, Pyrgo, and Lapwater,
And let them all to my elder daughter.
The rent I shall ask of her will be only
Each year's first violets. . . .

The series ends with the touching legacy to his wife:

And you, Helen, what should I give you?
. . .
Many fair days free from care
And heart to enjoy both foul and fair,
And myself, too, if I could find
Where it lay hidden and it proved kind.

All too often it had not proved kind, and the guilty knowledge of it made him even more exasperated and angry with himself and his family and their situation; so that he was either sullen or irascible at home, or went off for long periods, to be by himself and write or stay with friends and write—because he had lived all his life (since marrying the pregnant Helen when still at university) trying to make a living, never a comfortable one, by his pen. In the fifteen-odd years between coming down from Oxford and enlisting in July 1915 he wrote over thirty books, for the most part literary and literally potboilers, and reviewed at least that number every month. His publications included two volumes, *Oxford* and *Beautiful Wales,* in the handsome and much-collected "A & C Black Colour Series"; a good deal of nature and countryside writing of a kind that hardly exists anymore, having transferred to television; critical-biographical works on Keats, Lafcadio Hearn, Walter Pater, Maurice Maeterlinck, etc.; essays, and one novel, *The Happy-Go-Lucky Morgans.* That keeping the pot boiling was becoming next to impossible in the muted literary climate of the war years was a major factor in his joining the Artists' Rifles (the 22-year-old Wilfred Owen was part of the same intake) at the relatively advanced age of 37.

And it was from the Hare Hall camp in Essex that Thomas would walk over to nearby Upminster to visit an old friend of singular beauty, not seen in years, and not happily married, Edna Clarke Hall. Poor Helen had been abashed on meeting her during their first acquaintance around the turn of the century, later writing, "You came unexpectedly and had your arms full of autumn branches and I felt very shy of you because of your beauty and sweetness, because you had so much that because of my love for Edward I hoped to have": Of course modern criticism will not be having with us trying to tie love poems to real loves, though the Shakespeare of the Sonnets seems exempt from this stern rule.

However, given that, as I have said, there does appear to be a strong autobiographical element in Thomas's poetry and that this particular rainwalk is clearly especially talismanic to the poet, let's run with it just a little. First, here's another rain poem, finished only a fortnight earlier:

Like the Touch of Rain

Like the touch of rain she was
On a man's flesh and hair and eyes
When the joy of walking thus
Has taken him by surprise:

With the love of the storm he burns,
He sings, he laughs, well I know how,
But forgets when he returns
As I shall not forget her "Go Now."

Those two words shut a door
Between me and the blessed rain
That was never shut before
And will not open again.

Edna Longley, who has edited the exemplary and exhaustively annotated *Collected Poems* (Bloodaxe), suggests that this poem and "When We Two Walked" (written at about the same time) "may reprise the narrative of Hope Webb," an earlier extramarital dalliance terminated rather brusquely by the (much younger) woman's parents; but she does not appear to be aware of Edna Clarke Hall, who seems instead to be something of a coup for Matthew Hollis, in whose recent *Now All Roads Lead to France: the Last Years of Edward Thomas* (Faber), she looms quite large. Not that her existence was previously unknown, but he has got hold of her "journals and papers" (from "private hands"). I don't want to give the impression that ET was a relentless womanizer. In fact it is more than probable that his entanglements with both Webb and Clarke Hall were unconsummated: all the poems cited give the impression of a renounced might-have-been ("Go now"). I should perhaps add, none the less, that *Wikipedia* makes the surprising claim ("citation needed"), which I have not come across before, that Thomas fathered a child on his "housekeeper" (when could they afford one?), Anna Dineen, around Christmas 1914. (That the resulting daughter, born September 20th, 1915, should have been christened Helen almost beggars belief.) Perhaps the inevitable centenary biographies will cast further light, but in the meantime my confidence in my own claims for his chastity is ever so slightly rocked.

It would surely be hard to find a chaster image, though, than the closing one of "It Rains." Throughout Thomas's poetry, common roadside and hedge flowers are loved and named:

> Old Man, or Lad's-love—in the name there's nothing
> To one that knows not Lad's-love, or Old Man,
> The hoar-green feathery herb, almost a tree,
> Growing with rosemary and lavender.

(the opening lines of "Old Man," the fourth poem he wrote—only three days after the first: when the dam broke, it shattered. Thomas finished his first dozen poems between December 3rd and Christmas, 1914. Does this great outpouring make the Dineen story more, or less, likely?).

One is minded of Montale's "I Limoni":

> Ascoltami, i poeti laureati
> si muovono soltanto fra le piante
> dai nomi poco usati: bossi ligustri o acanti.
> Io, per me amo . . .
>
> (Listen, the prizewinning poets/ move only among plants/ with uncommon names: acanthus or box privet,/ I, for my part, love . . .)

You could hardly find a humbler flower than cow parsley, but Thomas makes of it an image of transcendent beauty. With their green stalks against a green ground hardly visible in the twilight, the white flowers seem suspended and ghostly in mid air: "The past hovering as it revisits the light." The past is always hovering around the edge of ET's poetry, its recollection as we have seen, the only happiness in the impossible present.

Actually Thomas was by all accounts capable of being excellent company in the here and now, even to his family, when things were going well, or less badly. I am going to avoid dwelling too much on the Edward Thomas-Robert Frost friendship. Whole books have been written on it, and doubtless there are more to come. Eleanor Farjeon in her memoir of their own friendship (*Edward Thomas: The Last Four Years*) has claimed that Thomas was already turning to poetry when he met Frost. However that may be, there is no doubt that Frost was a huge influence on the poet Thomas actually became. On their famous country walks, Thomas the strider over downs, Frost the pauser and leaner on gates, both unstoppable talkers, they together laid the ground for a twentieth-century poetry for normal human speech, a poetry that is the true ancestor of most of the decent writing since. When Thomas went to war Ezra Pound may have been yelling "Make it New!" but he was writing archaisms that read like stilted translations from the Provençal, even when they were not (*Hugh Selwyn Mauberley* was not published until 1920). To be fair, Eliot had "actually trained himself AND modernized himself ON HIS OWN," as Pound wrote to Harriet Monroe, recommending for *Poetry* "The Love Song of J. Alfred Prufrock," which Eliot had brought with him to England ready-made. But what has turned out to be the winning strain in English language poetry, the conversational, unrhetorical tone, goes back to these two, to Thomas and Frost. Not everyone has been happy, of course, with this tendency, which can to be sure produce dull enough poems in the wrong hands, and local outbursts of rhetoric and reaching-for-grandeur do break out in protest here and there and from time to time—Dylan Thomas being an obvious English or Welsh example. Auden, who bestrides twentieth-century verse like a colossus, is of course the main conduit, and recognized his indebtedness to Edward Thomas. This is what I meant by the not much aired specialness of Thomas, because although poets have been ready to acknowledge his paternity ("the father of us all"), it has been less readily conceded by the critics, with the honourable exception of F.R. Leavis.

As to grandeur, I have mentioned hitherto only Edward Thomas's as-it-were quieter poems, but there are one or two notable heavyweight pieces—tending to rhetoric, if you will—of which "Liberty" ("The last light has gone out of the world, except/ This moonlight lying on the grass like frost/ Beyond the brink of the tall elm's shadow . . .") and "Rain" are perhaps the best known. The last in particular is anthologized nearly as much as "Adlestrop," and committed to memory by schoolchildren (although that's perhaps too pious a hope nowadays: let's say "generations of schoolchildren" leaving it open whether the current one is to be included). Although much commented on, "Rain" isn't a poem that requires a lot of apparatus, except perhaps to say that Thomas was not a frivolous flirter with suicide, once indeed giving Helen a day of misery by storming out of the house with a pistol. One of the reasons he gave for failing to pull it off was the inability to enjoy it afterwards, the sloughing off of mortal care: not being able to say, to oneself or anyone, "Ah, that's done. Peace at last!" But it may be that his volunteering for active service with the Artillery (at his age he could have easily worked out the war as an instructor in the Artists' Rifles) was another roll of the dice.

Rain

Rain, midnight rain, nothing but the wild rain
On this bleak hut, and solitude, and me
Remembering again that I shall die
And neither hear the rain nor give it thanks

For washing me cleaner than I have been
Since I was born into this solitude.
Blessed are the dead that the rain rains upon:
But here I pray that none whom once I loved
Is dying tonight or lying still awake
Solitary, listening to the rain,
Either in pain or thus in sympathy
Helpless among the living and the dead,
Like a cold water among broken reeds,
Myriads of broken reeds all still and stiff,
Like me who have no love which this wild rain
Has not dissolved except the love of death,
If love it be for what is perfect and
Cannot, the tempest tells me, disappoint.

Amanda Luecking Frost

Triolets

— *Wea bið wundrum clibbor. Wolcnu scriðað*[1]

The grackle clacks its beak. What can't you say? Our woe clings. Silent clouds sweep over us. Light turns to darkness. Dark becomes the day. The grackle clacks its beak. What can't you say? The sky repeats the ocean's icy-gray, and wind sighs, blending water with the dust. The grackle clacks its beak. What can't you say? Our woe clings. Silent clouds sweep over us. Light turns to darkness. Dark becomes the day. Each echo hangs between us like the night, the knotted words the throat cannot unsay. Light turns to darkness. Dark becomes the day. Just as the owl dives quickly to its prey, the closing comes, the coolness of the bite. Light turns to darkness. Dark becomes the day. Each echo hangs between us like the night. The knotted words the throat cannot unsay. Woe lingers, and the clouds flash over us. The grackle clacks its beak. What can't you say? The knotted words the throat cannot unsay. Light turns to darkness. Dark becomes the day, the sweep of feathers in the flickering dusk, the knotted words the throat cannot unsay. Woe lingers, and the clouds flash over us.

1 Old English: Woe is wondrously clinging. Clouds glide by.
— *Cotton MS Tiberius B.i. (Maxims II),* British Library

Rachael Briggs

in the hall of the ruby-throated warbler

Jenny, sunny Jenny, beige-honey Jenny
sings the parsley up from the topsoil, Jenny,
cool tabouleh, hot apple crumble Jenny
alchemy Jenny

please, I whispered, *teach me the secret whistle*
help me coax the thistledown from the thistle
perch me on the branch where the goldfinch rustles
heedless of bristles

so she bore my heart to the eagle's aerie
folded me like down in a twig-tight nestle
kissed me till my sinews leapt up cat's cradle
brain like a beehive

Jenny, downy Jenny, my treetop lover
weave me in your goose feather arms forever

James Matthew Wilson

The Book of Nature II

The caterpillar grass
  Bleaches into its withered winter stasis;
The shadows of the fall's last spiders pass
  Into still, secret places.

Gravity has woven
  An umber bed of needles off the pines
That ring this acre, dried in a drought's oven,
  Which intimates some divine

Refusal to send rain.
  The needles pile like fingernails of those
Left, by authoritarian neglect, their pain,
  Their sweating woolen clothes,

To scratch at walls for seasons
  In the unworlded silence of a cell.
That is, the exercise of prowling reason
  Draws from this scene the hell

Of other days, discovers
  In the ashen curlicues of dormant vines
The nervous script of executed brothers
  Left dead along the lines.

This landscape is a poem,
    Forced back, retreated from the universe
To a depleted page's acreage, blown
    Into a hairline verse.

All that was once discerned
    In the created text of the plowed earth,
The rough-etched fractures of the sea, the turned-
    Out, sweetened afterbirth

Of isles of ripening fruit,
    Has been exiled. Appetite paves it over,
Erects a store for armaments or men's suits,
    Or a den for casual lovers.

Having such command,
    At last, imposing as he wills and does,
He makes a silent courtesan of the land
    To free her of other cause.

Despite him, reason seals
    This vision of a pine-ringed field within
The world as its indelible and real
    Mute book of blood and skin.

D.R. Goodman

Out Late in Summer

A glowing mist illuminates the street,
or so it seems, so magical the light
of street lamps on an August night. Not quite
thirteen, set loose, the freedom of bare feet
on pavement, buzzing insects, rare delight
of empty lanes, abandoned schoolyard, heat
and dark, forbidden smoke. Like cats, we meet,
assemble in the shadows, silent, slight
and furtive, keeping distance. But the thrill
of new connection flutters like the great,
bright Luna moth that flaps along the edge
of vision, brilliant, spinning in the thrall
of an imagined moon, quick like the heart
of someone poised for flight, perched on the verge.

D.R. Goodman

A Red-Tailed Hawk Patrols

Easy circles, yes, but never *lazy*—
Those lyrics have it wrong—each careless arc
An engine at its heart, a rust-red flame
Of blood-red purpose. How deceptively
She glides along; then, almost sleepily,
A half-shrug, quarter-wingbeat fuels a climb
Across the currents, past the ridgetop park
Where treeline disappears into a hazy
Gray of winter sky. She spirals back
With feathered legs suspended, searching eye
At work. How sweet the images we call on,
Of parachutes and gliders: human stock;
We dream ourselves beneath her wings and fly,
Forgetting beak, forgetting spur and talon.

D.R. Goodman

The Face of Things

The eye knows leaf from hummingbird at once,
Even at distance, even dusk; discerns
Among the flecks of green an immanence
Of sudden flight, as though the will returns

A subtle wavelength, visible as light.
The green of foliage, the leafy green
Of matching feather, then a clever sleight
Of surface that conveys a deeper scene,

The heartbeat underneath. The eye both *in*
And *measuring* the world—an inborn task
That even camouflage won't contravene
Cannot help pointing back behind the mask.

Depth cannot hide. And so it flutters, sings,
Betrays itself upon the face of things.[2]

---

2 "Technically adept, its other qualities—enlightenment; meaning that leads to more meaning—gained power with each re-reading. The hummingbird and its heartbeat reveal themselves to author and reader with something like joy. I say *joy* because it is presented here as a natural fulfillment, this desire that depth be known. This assertion that depth can*not* be *not* known. One may think of the depths of fine arts or the depth of a human soul or of cosmic depth: the poem gives rise to an epiphany that serves as a metaphor for so much. It's rather brilliant!"—Kelly Cherry, Final Judge, 2013 Able Muse Write Prize (for Poetry) on this winning poem, "The Face of Things" by D.R. Goodman.

David Mason

Out of the Marvelous: Remembering Seamus Heaney

. . . what's poetry, if it is worth its salt,
but a phrase men can pass from hand to mouth?
— Derek Walcott

Most important is to be able to enter a word like
a continent.
— Ted Hughes

Driving Seamus to the Denver airport in April 2001, I was a case of nerves. My hands had broken out in hives I prayed he didn't notice as I shifted gears and dodged the heavy traffic on the Interstate. Why I might be nervous around this most genial of men is a long story. He was the first poet I'd ever discovered on my own—in 1975, before he had a reputation in the United States—and his example had meant more to me than I could tell him.

In Colorado Springs two days before, I had taken him past the empty storefront that used to be the Chinook Bookshop. "That's where I ordered a copy of *North,*" I told him. "I was reading you before my professors." He hunched in the passenger seat, his quizzical expression warming at my recollection. That broad face with small pursed lips had become iconic. His tweed jacket and tie were the uniform one expected. But I hadn't realized his hands would not be a farmer's big claws. They were surprisingly refined. He had done his digging, as he promised in his most famous early poem, with a pen.

That night at dinner we had talked of mutual friends in Ireland, including Dennis

O'Driscoll, who would eventually die so much younger even than Seamus, and John Devitt, a marvelous Dublin teacher and raconteur, now also dead. It was John who told me in the 1990s my favorite Heaney story, one Seamus relished.

Driving some French friends down the Strand Road in Dublin, John had spotted Seamus walking and pulled his car over to say hello. Seamus leaned in at the window—that big squinting face in which you could see the farming lineage but also an atavistic, bemused intelligence. They chatted for a bit, and when Seamus went his way and John pulled into traffic again, his friends asked who that very nice man had been. "That man?" John always loved this bit: "That's the fucker who's gonna win the Nobel Prize."

Like so many others, I had my own anthology of favorite Heaney moments, all arising from the oral pleasures associated with his distinctively earthy voice. You can go back as far as "Digging" where a pen rests "snug as a gun," and where the work of shoveling spuds is described with such physical precision: "The coarse boot nestled on the lug, the shaft/ Against the inside knee was levered firmly." That *lug* rhyming with *dug* for me would always rhyme with *slug*, a word that crawled on the ground, one of the creeping things of creation itself. In the same famous poem a turf-cutter's motions are equally precise, the blade "Nicking and slicing neatly." No other recent poet has been so good at onomatopoeia. In the masterful title poem from his first book, *Death of a Naturalist* (1966), we find this image: "Right down the dam gross-bellied frogs were cocked/ On sods; their loose necks pulsed like sails. Some hopped:/ The slap and plop were obscene threats."

It's the mouthing of words, or words made flesh, he celebrates most, as in his love poem for his wife, Marie, "The Skunk": "The beautiful, useless/ Tang of eucalyptus spelt your absence./ The aftermath of a mouthful of wine/ Was like inhaling you off a cold pillow." Just saying the lines was more than half their meaning. Heaney gave (and gives) an aural fascination, but also an oral pleasure. You can play in his wordhoard (a noun he loved) like a kid slapping mudpies for fun. Leap ahead thirty years to his book *The Spirit Level* and you find the gift undiminished. No one has better described the work of a mason building a wall:

> Over and over, the slur, the scrape and mix
> As he trowelled and retrowelled and laid down
> Courses of glum mortar. Then the bricks
> Jiggled and settled, tocked and tapped in line.

The verse technique conveys a respect for the work, as if the mason's tocking and tapping were a kind of talking and measuring, a code like poetry itself. The poem pits that man's work against the destroyers, the killers, so it lives in a more rigorous moral realm than most contemporary writing.

The highway up the Front Range was not Colorado's beauty spot. I still feel apologetic when I take guests that way. We talked of literary things, mostly. Then, as if to check my local credentials, he asked, "That bird there—what would you call it?"

"A meadowlark," I answered. "You can tell from the yellow breast. They have the most beautiful song. Out in the prairies you can pull off the road and listen to them for hours."

"And those trees there?"

"Cottonwoods. See the line they follow—there's water there, maybe an *arroyo* or a small stream."

Arroyo. How far we were from Ireland. How far poetry had taken him, from the little farmhouse at Mossbawn to life as the world's busiest advocate for poetry, a man whose calendar was more jammed with speaking engagements than most politicians'. The story I heard in Ireland was that Marie had put a sign next to the telephone saying simply "No. No. No. No. No." It was not a word he used with any frequency.

Massive restrictions at security were not yet a part of our lives, but when I dropped him at the curb he reached into his luggage and brought out a bottle of Black Bush whiskey. "I don't suppose I can take this with me. You should have it."

It was talismanic. Seamus Heaney's whiskey! I drove back to Colorado Springs with a story to tell and a bottle I vowed I would never drink.

★★★

One of the first attempts at literary criticism I ever published was called "Seamus Heaney's Guttural Muse." It appeared in *The Mid-American Review* sometime in the 1980s and the editor put a typo in the title that has embarrassed me ever since. He called the essay "Seamus Heaney's Gutteral Muse." I remember seeing it spelled that way in the *MLA Bibliography* and thinking I would be cursed by the gods of typography. Somehow I was able to send the piece to Seamus with a handwritten correction and he sent a kind and complimentary postcard back.

The essay focused on his poem called "The Guttural Muse," in which the poet watches a scene in "a hotel car park":

> A girl in a white dress
> Was being courted out among the cars:
> As her voice swarmed and puddled into laughs
> I felt like some old pike all badged with sores
> Wanting to swim in touch with soft-mouthed life.

Now that I think of it, that early essay of mine also warned Heaney about fame. I took umbrage at Robert Lowell's comparison of him to Yeats and said Heaney reminded me more of Roethke. "Places great with their dead," Roethke had written, "The mire, the sodden wood,/ Remind me to stay alive." You could have told me Heaney wrote those words.

The conjoinment of public and private realms, the sense that history is personal and that one lives privately in relation to historical events, seemed significant. Richard Ellmann, in a piece contrasting the elevation of Yeats to the earthiness of Joyce, had placed Heaney in Joyce's camp, the way Joyce's characters are haunted by history. Others have noticed a similar earthbound influence from Kavanagh. All true enough. But when Heaney's great elegiac poem "Casualty" appeared in the *New Yorker* I clipped the pages, recognizing formal echoes not only of Yeats's "Easter 1916" but also of "The Fisherman." He was not so easy to peg.

Both *North* (1975) and *Field Work* (1979) are high points in the Heaney canon, but he never published a bad book. Time will pare away some weaker poems, some repetition, and will leave plenty of superior writing for readers to ponder and live with. Put succinctly, Heaney's problem after *Field Work* was to handle the earthward tug of autobiography in a new way, and also to find his own manner of transcending it.

★★★

The pull of the quotidian remained strong to the end. Seamus always wondered about the meaning of such matters, most famously in the tercets of *Seeing Things* (1991):

> The annals say: when the monks at Clonmacnoise
> Were all at prayers inside the oratory
> A ship appeared above them in the air.
>
> The anchor dragged along behind so deep
> It hooked itself into the altar rails
> And then, as the big hull rocked to a standstill,
>
> A crewman shinned and grappled down the rope
> And struggled to release it. But in vain.
> "This man can't bear our life here and will drown,"
>
> The abbot said, "unless we help him." So
> They did, the freed ship sailed, and the man climbed back
> Out of the marvelous as he had known it.

John Devitt once chided him for that lofty opening—"Hah! The annals say"—and Seamus gently but firmly put him in his place: "The annals *do* say it." He could cite chapter and verse. His scholarship was never slipshod, as he demonstrated in his translations and essays. There's a quality of mind in the poems as well, a grounded intelligence that allows for an intellectual life as well as a life of the body.

He transcended the quotidian by seeing it for what it is—the marvelous.

★★★

I first heard him read in Brockport, New York, back in the 1980s. He had a dental condition called "dry socket," and his hosts had left him on stage with a bottle of whiskey as pain killer. I needn't have worried—there was no drunken performance, but the measured and sane voice of a man happy to be there. After publishing that early essay, I corresponded with him a bit, and finally met him in Athens in 1997, when my friend Katerina Anghelaki-Rooke published a translation of his poetry into Greek. There was a reading at the Center for the Book with drinks afterwards on the roof. Seamus looked tanned and healthy, wearing a white linen suit that surprised me—it gave him an air of urbanity I hadn't known he possessed. But of course he was literally a man of the world by that time, and numbered among his friends the likes of Walcott and Miłosz, members in good standing of the Nobel Club.

I gathered the courage to introduce myself.

"We have a mutual friend, John Devitt in Dublin."

"Ah, John's a good man."

"Yes, we've spent many hours talking about your poetry."

That was it. Bango. He was whisked away to another engagement by Marie and friends. Later, a big party was held at the Irish Embassy and I foolishly did not attend, feeling there would be no real opportunity to talk to the man I had so long admired. What I heard afterward about that party suggests it would have been bibulous and fun.

When Seamus came to Colorado College at Easter 2001 (he read on April 16th, just three days after his birthday), he did not charge an exorbitant fee and gave generously of his time, talking to a class in aesthetics and to a faculty luncheon. The magic of the visit was that everyone seemed to get what they wanted. My colleague Jonathan Lee had the pleasure of hosting and introducing him. My friend Barry Sarchett took him to a local pub and arrived on the scene with a man as famous as Jesus. Every Irish nun in Colorado had come and brought their cousins too, and the church where he gave his reading, full at eight hundred people, was bursting with at least a thousand. My fellow poet Joan Stone and I got to see true eloquence close up.

In the classroom I asked him about his more exotic diction, not just Irish words, but the Latinate and Anglo-Saxon and Greek. "Are you a habitual reader of dictionaries?"

"No," he answered. His friend and former student Paul Muldoon was more that sort of poet. For Heaney words accrued from living. As he says in his *Beowulf* preface, the Anglo-Saxon word "thole," to endure, was common parlance among the Ulster farmers of his childhood. He had Church Latin as well as school Latin. The languages of work and play and even terrorism—words like "gelignite"—were the atmosphere of life.

As he stood before the faculty at lunch that day, he rocked momentarily on his feet and held the podium. "I think I'll begin by saying a poem to you, just to ground myself in the room and in the word before I speak." He recited from memory the Thomas Wyatt poem "Whoso List to Hunt," remarking on what seems estranging in the phrasing of it, and what becomes familiar—"I am of them that furthest come behind." And from this small harbor of familiarity he launched a shapely lecture on *Beowulf* and translation. Of course he was a practised speaker, one of the busiest on earth, and would have done versions of the same talk, the same reading, before. But he gave them the freshness of presence, the full joy of mouthing the words.

So why did I have a case of the hives? Why was I so nervous when we set out for the airport in Denver?

It was partly because I had written essays and reviews implying limitations in his work, and was afraid he would take offense. It was partly that he was the first poet I had found on my own; that I had learned from the example of his voice, had measured myself by the yardstick of his work ever since I first tried writing poems. And it was partly that I wanted him to love me as much as I had loved him, though I knew the desire was foolish and impossible.

At the curbside he gave me the talismanic whiskey.

The bottle stood on a shelf in my office for a week. Finally I thought, *Why not?* and had a few nips, holding the whiskey in my mouth and feeling the alcohol burn into my sinuses. I would go slowly. I would toast Seamus. I would taste the whiskey as I had tasted his words virtually all of my life.

Then, with the help of a friend or two, the whiskey was gone.

Alex Greenberg

At a Garden

I was sitting on a bench
dedicated to the death

of someone's husband.
I should have worn my suit for such an occasion.

Who knew it wouldn't be
just the pebbled ground again,

littered with offshoots,
the lilacs and the gardeners

of the Central Park Conservancy.
Today, as I am watching the yellow jackets

work through their orchids,
like one would a small necklace,

I wait for their gold bodies
to stain the mane of the flower.

But it never happens.
Even when I plunge my face

into the bloom and breathe
like someone's husband once did.

A man who never thought he would be
in memory of
at the Conservatory Garden.

Rachel Hadas

Remnants

A final burst of speed, and you were gone.
Your orphaned sneakers, metonymic last
vestiges of the long diminishment,
shirts, sweatpants—I retrieved these, lugged them home
to unpack, sort, repack, and give away.
So much else had long ago been lost:
purpose, focus, clarity, intent,
empathy, language, in the dryer tossed,
shrunken past use, past recognition. Now
let the lonely remnants follow too.

August '76: our first weekend.
You draped your work shirt like a thin blue friend
over a chair back and forgot it there
a little while, then asked "Where did it go?"
The question hangs unanswered in the air
thirty-five years later. Where are you?

Rachel Hadas

Mothers and Sons

A dingy farmhouse somewhere in Vermont.
Many small bedrooms on the upper floor.
All the doors are closed but none are locked.
I open each a crack,
peek in. In every room a double bed,
a tumbled quilt, walls of no color, day
leaking through the curtains. In each bed,
asleep, or not awake,
a mother and a son lie intertwined.
The mothers (I can see this at a glance,
however weak the light) are more or less
my age: not young. The sons,
grown up, have all gone far away, and now
come home if only long enough to eat
supper and go to bed
in their childhood rooms.

The faces, like all faces, are illegible in sleep:
in turn attentive, focused, blank, profound.
Perhaps each pair is dreaming of the journeys
that beached them there together bed by bed
if only for one night,
tangled in the breathing sheets, still warm.

Rachel Hadas

June Processions

Was it in a dream that I
accompanied an elderly
poet on a southbound train,
knowing we might not meet again?

What chilly wedding in the rain
(planned for a glass pavilion
but held inside a shadowy barn)
did I attend in early June?

One event succeeds another.
Show up, participate, retire,
then go back home and mull it over.
A visiting cousin tenderly

(he's eighty-five) embraces me,
knowing we may not meet again.
"Brave girl" is his valediction.
Courageous, neutral, cowardly,

I can't remember what I've done.
When did I lead a tearful ghost,
a poet fairly recently
gone, to a gallery redone,

changed beyond recognition—
the place, that is. Or I? Or he?
Next I witness a procession—
funeral, wedding, graduation.

Barefoot initiates make no sound
padding along the flowery ground
as birdsong drapes its canopy
over the path from A to B.

Dream hinge, ghost hinge, that separates,
just where they seem about to join,
event from expectation. . . .
Another wedding. It's late June.

In a floodlit atrium,
flowing-haired barefoot flower girls
are dancing long past their bedtime.
Hoping they soon can head for home,

yawning waiters clear the wine.

Catharine Savage Brosman

For a Singer Who Is Ill

— For S. K. F.

Yours is the gift of voice, of tone and ear,
the heavenly skills of Saint Cecilia,
by which celestial visions reach us here—
motets, *chansons* and *Lieder,* opera.

And yours is now the burden of disease,
not as the price of beauty—it is free,
if one consents to let the Muses please—
but as a warrant of humanity,

the terrible insignia of the Fall
when harmonies of body, torn apart,
became cacophony and funeral drum,

and led to elegy and mortal art.
You're tied to tubes, infusions, ports. Recall
your song; breathe soundly; let new music come.

Elise Hempel

Childhood

To shift all day in a zippered dress, then tear
from the brake of the bus, down the gravel drive, and leap
the back steps, slam the storm-door, take the stairs
two at a time, and fling the dress in a heap
on my bedroom floor, ease into my brother's old
T-shirt I'd saved from the Goodwill bag for mine,
frayed shorts, the torn red sneakers my mother had told
me to throw away, slam out again
and jump, both boy and girl, the chain-link fence,
just lie without a purpose in the loose
soft grass of the field, letting a garter snake glance
my hand on its passage, before my mother's voice
reached me, calling supper, and this list
of errands on a notepad, this watch on my wrist.

Melissa Balmain

Two Julys

Seven Months

By now the fireworks surely have begun,
the music and the battery of cheers—
too bright and loud for your new eyes and ears.
So here I stand, a mile from all the fun:
your body strapped to mine, as dense as stone,
I scan our patchy lawn. I smell a skunk.
I picture celebrating friends—free, drunk—
then stop and gape at what is ours alone.

Mere feet from us, across the cul-de-sac,
not near the grass the way they've always been,
but high among a neighbor's redbud trees,
salvos of lightning bugs flash gold on black.
You nestle silently beneath my chin
as we drink in the night's festivities.

Seven Years

The bugs are putting on a show again:
they glitter in a field of early corn.
We've come here, to the town where you were born,
in answer to your never-ending "When?",
your urgency to play where you once played.
Last night you twirled beneath unbroken sky.
A sparkler burned your thumb; you didn't cry.
You saw and heard the fireworks, unafraid.

Now as the insects loop-the-loop and blink,
you race with friends, too far away for me
to see the game or know if you're unharmed.
Some bugs, though separated, fire in sync—
like us, I tell myself, like family.
I wait beside the cornfield, empty-armed.

Chris Childers

Wedding Wings: A Toast

— *Book of Tobit 13:2*

WESTLEY: Can you move at all?
BUTTERCUP: Move? You're alive! If you want I can fly!
— *The Princess Bride,* William Goldman

If it ends with *mawwiage,* it's a comedy.
Let Buttercup and Westley stare
down Cliffs of Insanity,
Pits of Despair,
and death:
breath
sticks to his side,
the miracle is wrought,
plots unknot and the knot is tied.
It's inconceivable! Though also not,

since journeys to the bottom of the heart
are like that: storms and undertows
threaten to pull us apart,
the spirit grows
thin, ill,
until
the bitter weather
breaks halcyon, the dove
lends each earthbound soul a feather,
and, wing on wing, they climb the skies of love.

Each day can't be a comedy, it's true,
but can, with hope and help, fulfill
one heart dovetailed from two
by miracle:
today
I pray
love fills your cup
with grace in times of trial
and help and hope to lift you up.
Conceive it, and it's yours. The heavens smile.

— *For Patrick and Bethany, June 1, 2013*

Ancient Epithalamia: A Selection

Sappho

44

"Hector and company   are heading here now
from sacred Thebe   and Placia's slopes,
on board with playful-eyed,   pretty Andromache,
sailing her dowry   across the salt sea:
there's gold in abundance,   bracelets and bangles,
with royal robes,   beautiful baubles,
and countless cups   of silver, and ivories."
So the herald spoke.   Spryly, Hector's
beloved father   leapt to his feet,
and through the wide city   word went to friends.
The Trojans tied   mules to the traces
of carriage-cars   that glide in comfort,
and matrons and maidens   flocked to the feast.
Priam's daughters   processed apart;
young heroes yoked   horses to chariots. . . .

They entered Ilium   together, like gods.
The sweetness of pipes   and lyre-sounds swirled.
Castanets kept time.   Holy and clear,
the maidens' hymn,   more than human,

struck the skies.   In every street,
cups and pitchers   poured, and cassia
mingled its fragrance   with myrrh and frankincense.
Elderly women   whooped and warbled,
and all the fellows   in fine falsetto
called *Paean! Paean!*   *Lyre Player,*
awesome Archer!   So godlike Andromache
and Hector were hailed   in their wedding hymn.

104

O evening star, you bring home everything
the brilliant Dawn disperses as she warms;
you bring back sheep, and bring goats back, and bring
children back home into their mother's arms.

105a

An apple on a bough hangs redly, sweetly,
high on the highest limb, against the sky.
The pickers leave it be, but don't completely
leave it—they reached for it; it was too high.

105c

. . . a hyacinth, which shepherds in the mountains
trample, and the flower purples the ground. . . .

110a

The doorman's feet stretch seven fathoms;
five oxen died to make his sandals;
ten cobblers cobbled them together,
and it was hard work, too . . .

111

Carpenters, raise the roof up! There is—
        Sing *Hymen, Hymen!*—
    no room, no room.
The groom is coming, big as Ares—
        Sing *Hymen, Hymen!*—
    he's tall, this groom.

112

O husband, blessed now the request made in your prayers is granted—
the wedding's done; she's yours! You won the hand of the girl you wanted.
O bride, he'll prize your honeyed eyes, your body's pride and grace,
while Love's mystique flushes each cheek and streams from your beaming face,
for Aphrodite has made you mighty. . . .

114

Where, O where, Virginity, where have you gone, deserting me?
    I shall not come to you again; I shall not come again.

115

Bridegroom, how do you seem to me?
Just like a slender, sapling tree.

116

Honored guests, goodnight, and goodnight, bride.

141

The mixing bowl
stood there, brim-full,
and Hermes poured ambrosia round the room;
then the gods all
let offerings fall
from lifted cups, and drank health to the groom,
with every blessing.

— *Translated from the Greek of Sappho*
by Chris Childers

Idyll 18: Epithalamium of Helen and Menelaus

In Sparta, once upon a time, twelve girls—
the city's flower, the loveliest around—
with fresh-picked bluebells woven in their hair,
came to the home of golden Menelaus
to dance before his brand new bridal chamber,
when he, the youngest son of Atreus,
first welcomed in the wife he'd wooed and won,
Tyndareus's darling daughter, Helen.
They wove their steps together to the measure,
and sang this hymn, and all the house sang with them:

Hubby, in bed so early? What's this about?
You love your pillow? You're a lump of stone?
Or did one drink too many knock you out?
If you're so sleepy, you should sleep alone,
and leave the girl with girls her age, to play
till dawn, watched by the mother she adores,
since from now on, today and every day
forever, Menelaus, she is yours.

Some kind nose must have sneezed you victory
when you and all those heroes went to Sparta,
since only you joined Zeus's family,
and one sheet blankets you and Zeus's daughter,
whose rival never walked on Grecian soil.
How fine her children, if they're worthy of her!
When on the racetrack we all gleamed with oil,
just like the men, beside Eurotas river—
we four times sixty maidens, Sparta's pride—
not one seemed flawless, there at Helen's side.

Dawn's rising face is gorgeous, Lady Night,
and gorgeous, the white spring when winter's gone:
so golden Helen glimmers in our sight.
The corn adorns the field it's growing on;
a garden's lovely by its cypress-stand,
and chariots, by the horses they command;
so rosy Helen ornaments our land.
No spinner spins out yarn as fine as she;
no weaver with her shuttle engineers
or shears a more exquisite tapestry;
no one can hymn the Huntress or the fierce
warrior Athena, or strike the plangent lyre
like Helen, in whose eyes dwells all desire.

You're married now, O paragon of grace;
but we, in wreaths of flowers sweet with dew,
shall flock at dawn to the fields and the running place,
the whole time, Helen, thirsting after you,
as baby lambs thirst for their mother's breast.
We first will twine the wreath of melilot
to leave beneath the plane-tree's shady crest,
and first will sprinkle oil there on the spot,
tipping our silver flask beneath the tree,
and carve the plane bark with a Dorian
inscription for all passersby to scan:
it will say, "I am Helen's. Worship me."

New son of Zeus, farewell. Farewell, new bride.
May mother Leto grant your children health;
in Cypris be your shared love sanctified,
and Zeus, the son of Cronus, lavish wealth
unperishing from father unto son.
Sleep now, exhaling love and passion, breast
to breast, and don't forget to wake at dawn.
We'll be there too, when rising out of rest
the bard of birds with his wattled neck shall cheer.
Hymen O Hymenaeus, join us here.

— Translated from the Greek of Theocritus
by Chris Childers

62

It's Venus! On your feet, boys! Venus, long
awaited, crowns Olympus with her light.
The bride will come; we'll sing the wedding song.
Stop feasting and get up! The time is right.
Hymen O Hymenaeus, Hymen, come!

Girls, did you see the boys? Then on your feet!
It seems Mount Oeta sports the star of night.
You saw how fast they leapt out of their seat?
They leapt to sing; they're spoiling for a fight.
Hymen O Hymenaeus, Hymen, come!

To win the laurel, fellows, won't be easy:
look at them practicing what they've rehearsed!
They've got it down by heart. Yes, they've been busy—
no wonder, since they're utterly immersed.
Victory loves hard work, so they should smoke us.
We've listened, but we've been woolgathering.
Let's pull ourselves together now, and focus;
We'll answer them, and they're about to sing.
Hymen O Hymenaeus, Hymen, come!

Could heaven, evening star, burn crueler light?
You tear the daughter from her mother's arms
while the girl clings and holds her mother tight,
to serve her fervid husband with her charms.
What city's sack could be more cruel than this?
Hymen O Hymenaeus, Hymen, come!

Could heaven, evening star, show sweeter fire?
You seal betrothals when you shine your light,
betrothals both sides settled and desire;
our loves are joined when your flame climbs in sight.
What gods could give a more transcendent bliss?
Hymen O Hymenaeus, Hymen, come!

Ladies, the evening star stole one of us. . . .

. . . you rouse the guards you shine your light upon;
thieves hide at night, whom you come back and seize,
the evening star become the star of dawn.
But let them fabricate their gripes and taunt you;
so what? They chide, but silently, they want you.
Hymen O Hymenaeus, Hymen, come!

A garden wall surrounds a secret flower
which no herd tramples down, no plow destroys;
the breezes soothe it, sunshine feeds, rains shower,
and many girls desire it, many boys.
But when a nail deflowers it and shears it,
no boys or girls desire it any more.

Thus with virginity, while she reveres it;
but when it's plucked, and she's no longer pure,
no boys will speak to her, and girls are numb.
Hymen O Hymenaeus, Hymen, come!

A barren field bears an unmarried vine
that never climbs aloft or brings forth fruit,
but bends low with its brittle weight to twine
its stem-tip on the ground back to its root:
the farmers all, and all the steers, ignore it.
But if the same vine to an elm is wed,
the farmers all, and all the steers, care for it.
A virgin thus grows old, unhusbanded;
But when it's time to take the marriage oath,
she's loved by husband and by father both.

Now maiden, don't resist, and don't delay.
Don't fight the man your father gave you to—
your father and your mother—but obey.
Not all your maidenhead belongs to you;
One say's your father's; your mother has a say,
the third say's yours—don't fight the other two,
who dowered you and gave you to the groom.
Hymen O Hymenaeus, Hymen, come!

— *Translated from the Latin of Catullus*
by Chris Childers

Chrissy Mason

Salt Harvest and Flamingos: A Time in Lesvos

I think that someone will remember us in another time.
— Sappho (trans. Jim Powell)

Her voice came first.

Is that an Australian accent I can hear?

Mine came next.

What's an Australian doing in a shop in Molyvos market?

Which is, of course, a silly thing to say. I am there. Why wouldn't another Australian be? But her voice held something proprietorial which confused me. It was amused, calmly curious, whereas mine sounded simply astonished. Next, her head appeared through the wide-open door, and then the rest of her. Wavy brown hair, glints of red, small pale face; she looked young, but I knew she wasn't as young as all that. Old eyes. The look of having lost something and found something else. She was at home. And I was as far from home as I thought I could be.

Electra. I first met her name in Euripides' play during my final year of school near Melbourne, Australia. Later, at university, Freud gave me a different introduction. From myth, to complex, to immediate witness of a Greek woman explaining how her parents had emigrated to Australia where she was born. They worked hard for more than a decade, then returned to their village on Lesvos, with money behind them, when Electra was ten and without enough Greek to communicate with. Twenty-five years on, her strong Australian accent untarnished, and speaking Greek like the native she really is, she shared her story as we drank thick sweet coffee at a table on the cobbled lane outside her shop, while she made fine brush-strokes on a plate. She is a ceramic artist, and sells her hand-painted pottery in the Molyvos (ancient Mythimna) historic market which is completely screened from the hot sun by arm-thick, twisted vines of wisteria.

The island of Lesvos was to be our last stay in the Greek adventure I knew I would have one day. The culture of Greece—its literature and philosophy, its olives and feta and yoghurt, its Pascha with the bells and the red eggs and spiced bread and marinated lamb—thrives in Melbourne where I come from. Melbourne has the second largest Greek population in the world after Athens. The cities share a degree of latitude (37N, 37S), a climate, and a particular blueness of sea and sky. After my own name, the name of the tree thriving in many parts of Greece would have been among the first Greek words I learnt to say—*eucalyptus.*

Soon, Yiorgos joined us. *Your name means pure gold,* he said to me, and the jokes flew across the narrow cobbled lane as we played between each other's languages. Yiorgos owns the nearby jewelry shop where I'd bought blue butterfly earrings two days earlier. Spring in the Mediterranean is alive with butterflies. During our time in Crete and the Peloponnese, the fields flared with wildflowers and the rootless flowers of the air, the *petalouda*—in a lyrical Greek analogue, a butterfly is a "flying flower." While hiking on the Delphi path high above the Temple of Apollo, chasing an elusive, living version of the earrings in Yiorgos's window display, another solitary walker paused to tell me about the Valley of the Butterflies on the island of Rhodes. I need to go there one day. When I met Yiorgos, we bargained over the tiny silver and blue counterfeits I wanted, for remembrance, and he didn't give way. But of himself he gave largely and freely. When he spoke to me in Greek, he spoke slowly and so clearly that my eyes darted with recognition, the Greek words brushing on my brain like blue butterfly wings; I would catch a glimpse of a root-word, then fail to grasp the word as a whole. Many Greeks speak good English. Only their delight in expanding my vocabulary and laughing at my barbaric grammar spared me the shame of my own monolingualism. By the time I left Greece, I had a delicious, thwarted feeling of being almost possessed of what I do not own. Its language winks at me.

And my name, said Electra, *means amber. It's the ancient word for the sun, for flow, and the root of the modern word—electricity. I've always wanted a piece of amber.* Thales, in 600 BC, noticed how bits of straw clung to rubbed amber. Static electricity. When Electra longed for amber, my wrist reached out to her. On it, a chunk of amber hung from a slender strip of leather. All my life I had wanted amber, too. And in another artist's shop in Nafplio, the first capital of Greece, I had found a piece I could afford. Electra touched it with her eyes, and then her fingers. In that moment, I knew it belonged to her. As soon as we parted that day of our first meeting, I slipped it off my wrist and carried it in my pocket, waiting for an opportunity to press the amber bracelet into her hand.

And my name, Yiorgos went on, *means George.* At that, we all laughed loud enough to bring Maria out of her café to proclaim that the loudest tourists in the world are Australians, give me a bosomy hug, and refill our coffee cups. This time, Yiorgos wasn't fooling me. I knew his name derives from "earth," and apt it is. Gardener, caretaker, businessman, artist, drawn equally to community and solitude, arms as big and warm as an entire island of olive groves, it was Yiorgos who told me about Electra's singing.

She sings the old songs, the songs of Asia Minor, he said. *Her voice is very good, very beautiful.*

My father taught me, she said. *I loved to hear him sing, and sang along with him. In August, this place is filled with music. Musicians come, and play the traditional songs. Last year, for the first time, I sang here with Solon Lekkas.*

I stared. *Solon was here? You know Solon? You sang with him?*

She nodded, a quiet smile. *I learnt so much from him, so much.*

What? What did he tell you? I wanted to know.

He didn't tell me anything, she said.

★★★

A few days before I met Electra, our group had driven from Molyvos to Mytilini where Solon Lekkas lives. Renowned in Greece as a singer of the traditional songs of Lesvos and Asia Minor, Solon came into our lives accidentally, if you believe in accidents. One of our party had stumbled on a recording of Solon singing on *YouTube*. On first hearing the sound he produces, all one's veins and arteries tighten and vibrate like strings. Now we were traveling to see a live performance arranged through a series of serendipitous encounters, the kind that make travel so seductive.

Halfway along the road to Mytilini, the rocky, forested hills descend to the salt pans of Kalloni and the largest wetland area in Greece. We drove past these wetlands at sunset, past mounds of stockpiled salt glaring white like volcanic peaks. The wetlands draw people from all over the world to see and hear birds such as crested larks, black storks and pink flamingos. Over one hundred different bird species have been recorded at Kalloni, some previously thought to be almost extinct. A system of evaporative pools produces each year tons of salt reputed to be the whitest in all Europe. The symbiotic relationship between modern solar salt production and the creation of bird habitat is marvelous to see. In fact, it was here in the lagoon of Kalloni that Aristotle did the biological work for his *Historia Animalium,* or History of Animals. But on this particular and glorious evening our thoughts were pushing further up the road towards our meeting with Solon Lekkas.

In promotional text for concerts, Solon talks about the history of the traditional music of Lesvos, and its irresistible communicative power:

> In Lesbos we have the aman songs, the old karsilamas songs and the heavy zeibekiko. You don't find those in other places, only here. We always had them. It is our tradition. The people that came from Asia Minor, when they came, they found these songs here. We already had them. You know, Lesbos and Turkey were really one and the same; Lesbos and Aivali, there was a continuous coming and going between us. The same habits, traditions, clothing you could see in Lesbos, Aivali, Pergamon. The men here always sang amanedes, even when singing for a girl in the morning, they would sing an aman song. In the old times the people would always dance and party with the music, usually in couples. Two men would dance together the karsilamas, the zeibekiko, the sirtos, so as to look at each other and communicate with the dance.

This quote is a translation. Solon doesn't speak English. A fragment of Sappho crossed my mind as Solon and his three musicians, including his fourteen-year-old grandson on bouzouki, brought the taverna to life:

> Surpassing, like the singer of Lesbos, those elsewhere. . . .
> — Sappho (trans. A.S. Kline)

Another translation, of course. Sappho has poured herself through language and time to be present to my mind on such occasions. Here was that singer, singing in a language I didn't understand, in another kind of language I *did* understand. Solon laid down his lore. Yearning, lewd, hilarious, telling stories of wine, fishing, sex, harvest, voyages, his songs pulled back the arbitrary folds of time. We were all transported into the moment. And when he got up to dance, his body did not leave the ground. The ground is what he touched, repeatedly, his touchstone. The room warmed, ululated, and everybody danced. There was no conversation, yet everything got said. We were heady with clarity. And Solon leaned back, that quiet smile, and the constancy of the ouzo glass and the cigarette at his lips and of his fingers clicking his komboloi.

Two days later, on April 25th, we made the hour-long ferry ride from Mytilini to Ayvalik in Turkey. A retinue of gulls, flying level with our heads at arm's reach, escorted the ferry from Greek waters. We spent the day wandering the Acropolis and the Sanctuary of Asklepios at the site of the ancient Greek city of Pergamon. Gypsy children flying a homemade paper kite into the air above the Acropolis made light of the weight of stone and history. These Aegean places live in the ceaseless commerce between cultures, and between past and present, each influencing each other's architecture, art, food and music. Places like Lesvos and Bergama are so distinctive, yet so connected to each other, that the notion of boundaries is obviously a nonsense. Borders are political, and can be dangerous things. Culture—like amber, or like thyme honey, or mountain tea, or the singing of Solon Lekkas—flows, creating vitality through touch. Many of Sappho's verses resound with a desire to be influenced. That's what love is.

War, too, loosens bonds, allowing cultures to affect each other. April 25th is Anzac Day, and as the bus took us back to Ayvalik to catch the returning ferry, I saw road signs indicating Gallipoli was barely two hours north, and I knew over five thousand Australians and New Zealanders were gathered at Anzac Cove. And I longed to be there with them. As we sailed back to Lesvos, I showed Atatürk's "Letter to the Anzac Mothers, 1934" to the group of American students we were traveling with.

> Those heroes that shed their blood and lost their lives. . . . You are now lying in the soil of a friendly country. Therefore rest in peace. There is no difference between the Johnnies and the Mehmets to us where they lie side by side now here in this country of ours . . . you, the mothers, who sent their sons from faraway countries, wipe away your tears; your sons are now lying in our bosom and are in peace. After having lost their lives on this land they have become our sons as well.

They had not heard the Anzac story, and were unaware of its significance in Australian culture. The commerce between Australian and Greek/Turkish culture made travel in Greece especially easy for me; most Greeks I met had relatives in places I know well, and had either visited Australia or lived there for a time, so we were soon hugging due to this mutual recognition. I was also fortunate to be traveling with a husband who speaks Greek as the Greeks speak it. Nonetheless, I still hear Yiorgos saying, over and over, *Language is not a barrier. You know who a person is, in their heart, you just know.* I heard this so often in Greece, from taxi drivers and shopkeepers; from Greeks who had left their country and come back, and those longing to leave; from the old woman who had never left Molyvos and blessed us at the harbor, *kalo sta paidia*—good to the children. When people dance together and look at each other, you know them.

Not long after a sailor replaced the Turkish flag with a Greek one on the boat deck without any fuss, the statue of Sappho came into view above Mytilini harbor like a beacon to our progress. This is the best way to view the town's prominent feature from every angle: to approach it from the sea. What does she hold above her head so high? I couldn't tell if it was a torch or a garland of flowers. But I can say getting back to Lesvos was sweet, and knew it would be bitter to leave, and I thanked her inwardly for the thought that came directly from her. For Sappho of the two minds, and Sappho of the quiet mind, perhaps the torch and the flower are one and the same.

★★★

Our last few days in Molyvos passed as dreams do. The busy brain goes drowsy as the Mediterranean summer heats up. We swam in water so salty it pushes back when you dive into it. I found unusually-colored sea glass on the pebbled beach; found the best flavors of our Greek sojourn at Roula's fish restaurant—fresh octopus with rocket salad—on the seductive harbor front; found myself more at home than anywhere I have ever been; and found Electra's hand and pressed the amber bracelet into it.

On the way to Mytilini airport, our bus was stopped for some time as a fleet of trucks carrying salt took its right of way through a narrow village street. After the salt harvest, villagers will continue to pick the whitest sea salt in Europe from the salt flats as they have done for centuries. And the pink flamingos will stand in the pools, and the villagers will know the lyrics to the life-songs of their people because they are not afraid to go there, to the warm, dark gut of their culture. As I watched the trucks pass, marveling at the sight of so much salt, I thought of a poem by Yannis Ritsos, translated by my husband, David Mason.

> Lean girls are gathering salt on the shore,
> bending to bitterness, ignorant of the open sea.
>
> A sail, a white sail, beckons from the blue,
> and what they do not see in the distance
>   darkens with longing.

I never went to Eressos, the Lesvos town where Sappho might have been born, might have lived. Before arriving in Lesvos, I had thought I needed to go there, for the frisson of connection to the essential Sappho in the place most associated with her. Leaving Venice a week later, after five remarkable days there before heading back to the US, I realized my husband and I must be among the few visitors to that city who never stepped into St. Mark's Basilica or the Doge's Palace, and I started thinking about how our travels often don't take us where we think we want to go.

Travel is a little like tragedy in that sense, one of the ways purpose can be deflected, and we can be turned aside from the self we imagine we are and from the objects we think we desire, and be opened to a new vision. Sappho's famous prayer to Aphrodite characterizes the goddess as reluctant to give satisfaction to the supplicant, or at least playful about her plans for delivering it. I wonder if salt provides an insight to the complexity of desire. Salt, that paradox, a magnet to moisture maintaining its dryness. Where does the water go? It goes into keeping desire for itself alive. The residue of salt is the sweetness of longing.

Perhaps Sappho lives everywhere we never go. Yet I sensed her softness in the wooded hills, the open wetlands, the panoramic view from Ypsilou monastery where sea and sky drop all pretense of being separate, and in the sound of the lark humming the evening air.

Sometimes, the pink flamingos are not visible on the salt pans. Their color is almost empty. Everything evaporates. Even pink. What remains on the earth when the sun is done is salt-stained. The bus turns away from the constant, lively heart of Mytilini towards the airport. And as the figure of Sappho high above the harbor bends from sight for the last time, I clasp my bare wrist in a sign of trust. And Electra, holding her own, says, *You've been here before. You'll be back again.*

Stephen Harvey

Last Dance

With Hanna barely old enough to walk
And you just young enough, both of you clung
In playful counterbalance to your cane,
Weaving through the living room among
A dozen arms readied to intervene.
And neither of you bothered to explain
The secret of the century between
An old man and a girl; you didn't talk

About the wisdom middle age obscures,
For all that we could notice was the sum
Of years—though ninety-nine of them were yours,
Her only one kept close, as if she knew
By some familiar sense of peace that you
Would leave reluctantly, as she had come.

Jeanne Wagner

"The Unfaithful Shepherd"

— By Pieter Breughel

(with quotes from Boris Pasternak)

His brash tights tell the whole story:
a taste for the garish, a longing
for some lost *joie de vivre*
that's settled down
into the swollen red sacks of his hose.
See how they run—
lift and run as he goes,
legs pounding like blood,
carrying the doughy bulk of his body,
a smile on his broad peasant face.

Because this is homily, Brueghel inclines
the bare field downward,
gravity like sin,
the ground rutted with last night's rain;
its tracks arrowing the direction
the poor shepherd's fleeing in.

His sheep too are running away,
their bodies soft white blurs of flight,
like angels ascending into callous air.

Now look to the right,
the wolf's already there,
his muzzle stuck in the soft bowel
of a newborn lamb.
Whoever said, *to live is not as easy*
as to cross a field
must have known about nights
surrounded by the warm fug of animal breath,
where the wolves await, patient as death.
Their persistence another kind
of faith.[3]

---

3 "I admire all the descriptions in this poem, find the Pasternak quotation ironically appropriate, and was stunned by the wolves at poem's end. This poem is a wonderful ekphrasis and makes the reader look harder at the painting."—Kelly Cherry, Final Judge, 2013 Able Muse Write Prize (for Poetry) on this second-place poem, "'The Unfaithful Shepherd'," by Jeanne Wagner.

Cheryl Diane Kidder

How the West Was Won

After

Tired. Barely awake. Finally getting a ride home. We're silent in the car. It's fall. Mornings are close to freezing. My blue dress with the bell sleeves is ripped. Pantyhose gone. I'm not recognizing any roads. He turns on the heater. He lifts the hem of my dress and puts his hand on my leg. I start shivering. He says, Relax. I pull away from him. I say no for the millionth time. He reaches into his jacket pocket and pulls out something shiny, metal. There's a pop and it turns into a knife. He lays the blade on my leg where his hand used to be. He's driving on the freeway with one hand. I catch myself not breathing.

Much Earlier

Poor Little Rich Girl. We've watched it before and when it comes up again I know all the songs by heart. Shirley lives in a big beautiful house with her father. She has a collection of porcelain dolls as big as she is, from all over the world. Her clothes are silk and taffeta. One day, she goes on an adventure and ends up living with the organ grinder. He's Italian and has a big family. They eat spaghetti all the time. They always have an extra place at the table. Meanwhile, her father is frantic to find her.

Before

We're in a club listening to a new band. If Tim likes them, he'll book them at the university. We came in early. Got a table up front. Introduced ourselves to the band. Met the sound guy and the manager. The first set was great. I wanted to dance. Tim didn't. I ordered a beer. Tim didn't. While the band took a break, Tim went to talk to the manager. The sound guy came over to our table and invited us to a party after the show. He said if we didn't want to drive we could get a ride from him. He drove the equipment truck and there was plenty of room.

Much Earlier

I never missed my favorite TV show *The Girl from U.N.C.L.E.* on Tuesday nights. U.N.C.L.E. stood for United Network Command for Law Enforcement. Stephanie Powers was April Dancer: fashion model by day, undercover agent by night. She wore white go-go boots and patent leather miniskirts. Her partner was Mark Slate. When they needed to talk to each other they used communicators that looked like pens and carried small devices that looked like my turquoise transistor radio. Sometimes she wore patent leather caps that matched her skirts. She had long dark hair and wore heavy eyeliner. She was always getting Mark out of trouble. She was in charge.

Just Before

Tim refused to go to the party. I told him I really wanted to go. He'd already accused me of turning into an alcoholic when he saw me having a second beer earlier, so it didn't surprise me that he wanted to go home. I told him it wasn't fair. I told him I wanted to go. We stood outside the back door of the club arguing as the band loaded their equipment. The sound guy walked by and offered us a ride again. I told Tim I was going and walked off to the equipment truck hoping Tim would stop me, follow me, grab my arm, say something. I was all the way to the passenger seat of the truck before I turned around. All I saw was Tim driving off in his blue Valiant. I stepped into the truck and shut the door behind me.

Much Earlier

How the West Was Won was the first film I ever saw. It was a Western. It was really four Westerns in one film and it had more stars in it than any other film I'd ever heard of. It was filmed in PanaVision which filled up the movie screen with so much wide open space, you felt like you were right there in the movie with the actors. You were shooting down the rapids with the pioneers, you were galloping through the deserts and the forests with the mountain men, you were playing poker on the steamboat when Debbie Reynolds falls in love with the man who will leave her. And forever after, the song she sings as a grandmother to her three grandchildren, *Shenandoah,* will be the song you hear in your dreams, will mean the future is wide open, will mean you can be anything you want to be, will mean you will survive hardship and prosper and people will love you and you will have a happy life. And when you're not even thinking about it, when you're cooking dinner, or driving to work, when you first get up in the morning, or are in the shower, the melody will work its way back to you, only sad this time, and you won't know why.

A Little Earlier

I had no idea where the sound guy was going, but the guitarist's girlfriend had come along in the truck and she was very chatty and very blonde. I liked her. Seemed like we drove for an hour out of town. I focused on Sally's voice and her stories of traveling with the band all over the state, how she'd skipped work and school to be with her boyfriend and how they were planning on getting married and how she couldn't wait to have children. She knew they would be musical.

An hour later Sally and I were rolling around on the couch in the living room, giggling, watching *Straw Dogs* on TV, covering our eyes when the gang of roughs breaks in and attacks Susan George, coughing from all the smoke, falling off the couch and not bothering to yank our skirts back into place. Sally said she had to pee and grabbed my hand.

She sat on the toilet and I stared at myself in the mirror. My hair was a mess, my lipstick completely gone. I opened up a bathroom drawer at random but found only razors and soap, toothpaste and shoe strings in little packages. I took the tube of toothpaste out and squeezed some on my finger, then leaned in to the mirror and brushed my teeth with it. It tasted gritty.

Sally was throwing up behind me. I asked her if she needed any help and she just groaned. I wasn't sure what to do, so I sat on the floor and held her hair back. Her dress had slipped off her shoulder and was hanging around her waist. When she was done, she sat back on the toilet. Her eyes were closed. I pulled the straps of her dress back up over her shoulders and asked her if she wanted to stay there or go back into the living room. She said she'd stay there for awhile and slightly bowed her head. Her hair fell like a curtain.

Much Earlier

One Sunday, right in the middle of Shirley Temple Theater, I looked outside and saw snow falling. Snow in Cupertino is a once in a lifetime event. I jumped up, even though *Poor Little Rich Girl* was just about my favorite episode, put on my slippers and went for the front door.

Mother stopped me, insisted I put on a sweater. Father got up off the couch and we walked outside onto the front porch. All our neighbors were out as well. The sun was shining and everything was covered in white. Of course everyone had a big front lawn. Now, all the lawns were vast expanses of snow. There was just enough for it to stick. I ran out into the middle of it and reached down with my bare hand to pick it up. I tried to roll a bunch of the stuff into a snowball. My hands turned bright red. I threw it up in the air and it all fell away, powdery and glistening, back onto the lawn. My hands were cold, my slippers were wet and all the way down the street, every neighbor kid was doing the same thing, parents standing up on their porches watching, kids running around making footprints in the new snow. I'd never seen anything so beautiful.

During

The guitarist was so cute. He had long blond hair, like his girlfriend, cut in a shag and he moved so well on stage. Didn't hurt he was a great guitarist, but it was his singing that really got to me. He had that kind of rock voice, hard and raspy.

I knew Sally was indisposed in the bathroom and I'd seen the guitarist go into the bedroom with at least two different women from the party. I wandered back into the kitchen and picked up a new drink, something in a glass with a lime in it. It didn't taste too much like alcohol so I had a couple.

I wandered back into the living room. *The Getaway* was on TV. I loved Steve McQueen. I sat in the corner of the couch and watched bodies rolling around on the carpeted floor in the dark, under a strobe light. Then the light turned into a bunch of different colors. I put my head back on the couch and watched them dancing on the ceiling. Someone took my hand.

I looked up. It was the guitarist. I got up and followed him into the bedroom. He sat me down on the bed and walked out. The sound guy came in and closed the door behind him. I heard the click of a lock on the door, but from the outside. I thought that was weird.

The sound guy sat down next to me and put his arm around my shoulder and asked me if I was having a good time. I told him I was and asked when the guitarist was coming back. He said, in just a couple of minutes, why don't you lie down for a while and wait?

It felt good to lie down. The room stopped spinning. He took my shoes off. I pushed myself up on the bed so I could have a pillow under my head. I almost closed my eyes. He reached up under my dress, the blue one with the bell sleeves, and grabbed the top of my pantyhose and pulled them down. He told me to lift my hips to make it easier. I lifted my hips. It felt much better to lie there without shoes and pantyhose. I almost closed my eyes. He lifted my dress up over my head, my blue dress with the bell sleeves, but I told him no, I don't want to do that and pulled it back down. He yanked it up again and tried pulling off my underpants. I pulled his hand away, told him to stop it and rolled toward the edge of the bed. I was afraid my dress would rip. My sleeve was caught under his arm. I didn't want to yank too hard, it was my favorite dress. He grabbed my shoulder and pulled me back on the bed facing him. He told me to stay put. He told me I was not leaving the room any time soon. I looked into his eyes, put my hand on his face and tried to push him away. He grabbed my arms and pinned me down on my back, spread my legs with his knee and pulled my underpants to the side. I twisted away but I was so tired. I was tired. I wanted to go to sleep. He pressed in on top of me. He was bent, crooked. It had never occurred to me that they could be crooked. I knew what was happening then. I stopped moving. I went limp. The bedroom door opened and the drummer walked through the room and disappeared into the bathroom. I said Hey, in my head, but it didn't come out of my mouth. I heard myself grunting, I heard myself catching my breath, trying to get a breath, he was so heavy on top of me, his beard, my blue dress, please don't rip my blue dress, the bed was the biggest bed I'd ever seen, I was lost, I couldn't see the edge any more, I couldn't see anything but his hair in my face, his breath on my neck, I was so tired, I wanted to close my eyes, I wanted to go home, but I was lost, so lost, his belt buckle digging into my thigh, his boots crushing my feet, the loud smell of aftershave, beer and pot on him, just wanted to go home, wanted to stop, wanted this to stop, stop now, don't rip my blue dress.

Much Earlier

April Dancer was kidnapped by T.H.R.U.S.H. agents. T.H.R.U.S.H. *(Technological Hierarchy for the Removal of Undesirables and the Subjugation of Humanity)* was the evil organization that all U.N.C.L.E. agents were sworn to stop. Mark Slate had to swoop in and, uncharacteristically, save her. They had placed her in a rolling desk chair binding her ankles and wrists with rope and wrapping a scarf around her mouth so she couldn't scream. Then they left her alone. But they hadn't counted on her U.N.C.L.E. training. She knew how to bite through a gag, untie the most complex knots and bust out of a locked room using the quarter-sized bit of nitroglycerin secreted into the heel of her go-go boot. Just as she had successfully blown through the steel door of her prison, Mark shows up, gun in hand, completely unnecessary, with a look of great disappointment. April runs past him, yelling for him to keep up, the T.H.R.U.S.H. agents were getting away. Mark shrugged his shoulders and took off after her, sporting white shoes, a white belt on his corduroy bell bottoms and a jaunty white cap. But April Dancer didn't need anyone to rescue her. She was The Girl from U.N.C.L.E.

After

She spent the last part of the drive home with her head in his lap, the knife, cold, on the back on her neck. Every few seconds she choked on it, but he'd take his hand off the wheel and push her head back down. She thought she might throw up. She wished she would throw up.

She felt the car slow down. They were pulling off the freeway. Maybe it would be better to get out here, a couple miles from home, so he didn't have the exact address. Had she already given him the exact address? She made a move to sit up but he pushed her down again, pushing the knife harder into her neck so she could feel its point.

Just as the car pulled to a complete stop he pushed her off of him and she sat up. He didn't zip up, just pulled his shirt down. She sat frozen in the front seat of the equipment truck. She looked down at his hands but no longer saw the knife.

What are you waiting for? he said.

She looked up. They were parked in front of her house. The house she shared with Tim. It was early, but the sun was up. She looked through the front window, hoping no one was up yet. She put her hand on the door handle and hesitated. He reached across her and threw the door open. She wanted to get out as fast as she could, but her legs were stiff from being in one position, everything seemed to hurt. She rolled her legs out first, then stood up outside of the car, not really sure he was going to let her go. He reached across the seats, closed the door and pulled away from the curb. She was standing in the middle of the street in her blue dress, holding her shoes.

Now

Now, right now, walking up to my house, I realize I don't have my keys. I knock softly a couple of times. Tim answers the door. He just stands there in the front hall staring at me. I walk past him and go into the bathroom.

I'm shivering. I take everything off and grab my robe, walk back into the bedroom. He's sitting up in bed. He won't say anything, doesn't even ask me where I've been, what happened, what had I been doing, who drove me home. I know what he's thinking just by looking at his face.

What do you care? I ask him. You don't love me. Why do you care at all that I didn't come home?

I couldn't cry. He doesn't want to know where I'd gone, what I'd done. He assumes he knows what happened.

I walk over and sit on the bed next to him. He puts his arm around my waist. I put my head on his shoulder.

Much Earlier

When we came back into the house, shivering from the snow, Shirley was just being reunited with her father. He had found a new wife while looking for Shirley and she was thin and blonde and kind. Now Shirley would have the family she'd always dreamed of. They all sang a song. But my favorite part was Shirley sitting on the floor in her bedroom with all her porcelain dolls sitting around her. She sang to each one in a different accent as each doll was from a different corner of the world. One day, I thought, I will visit all the places her dolls are from. I knew that anything was possible, that the future was wide open before me, that I could be anything I wanted to be, that every day would have a happy ending.

Tara Tatum

The Nut House

You know how writing conferences go:
there's a whole lot of ass kissing, in more
ways than one. That is, with amateurs,
it's figurative, and with the older,
greater writers, literal—ass kissing.
How ironic, right? They've had enough
of metaphors and irony and talk
of pedantry, thinking even, and want
to feel some juicy, young lips on their asses.

This is a true story. I swear. Last year
I went to the *Langdon Review* in Texas
(see pure facts here, no disputing them)
and a friend invited two writers (for legal
reasons I will not provide their names),
apparently "distinguished" writers, hell
if I know, to our pool. Well, I was wearing
one of those tight bikini bottoms,
like boy-cut underwear, where your ass cheeks
hang out this perfect way that thins your legs
but shows the bottom half like some plump fruit
you want to suck the juice from.

My mistake,
those shorts, I'm sure of it. But then again,
it probably would've happened still.
It's not a big deal (it could've been, depending . . .).
This one writer, my grandpa's age, struck up
a conversation, all bullshit at first,
asking what I wanted out of life,
as if he cared, me asking him where he taught,
what he wrote, as if I cared; then he grabbed
my naked leg. He caressed it, mostly. God,
some older men have no restraint. There are
younger girls who don't believe (not always)
a sticky night will always get you published—
I thought he used to always get his ass kissed.

I played it cool. You play it cool after
you drink a bottle of whiskey, one of those
"I might puke if I get too worked up" cools.
He wasn't creepy, though. He had these bright
blue eyes and tanned skin and real rough hands
(I love rough hands—I love contrasting skins)
and had aged well. He had. And for a second
I wanted to sit on his lap. I get those urges—
to straddle laps—my body melts in sweat.
It's the closest thing to safety that I've felt.

But this is what got me: his hotel's name:
The Nut House. Honestly, The House of Nuts.
Swear to holy acorns, look it up.
Granbury, Texas. So, Mr. Blue Eyes
asked me if I wanted to go there
to stay with him. He was a serious writer
and had a wife and kids. I'll never marry
a serious writer. The House of Nuts
is the only place I imagine writers staying.
The nuts who crack from stresses of a hand—
The sagging nuts, the nuts filled up with seeds,
the nuts who fall from trees into a lap.
Look it up. In Granbury. Go stay there.

Matthew Buckley Smith

Requited Love

Here is the way they rose and bathed and fed
In silence, and in silence got undressed,
And microwaved the supper each thought best,
And meant the words the TV actors said;
Here is her naked hand outstretched in bed
To soothe some restless memory's knocking chest,
And here her present body, seldom pressed
Awake to his, and here his snoring head;
Here are the things they thought they had to fear:
The figure at the far end of a glance,
The skulls a little clearer every year,
The lovely hair's retreat, the veins' advance,
Neglected taxes, mice, the common cold,
Shares held too long, the child they'd never hold.

Richard Wakefield

Keepaway

The playground hosts a noontime game today.
The fattest kid in school is forced to chase
his lunch bag in a game of keepaway.
He lumbers side to side across the space
the laughing crowd has cleared, no breath to plead
with this boy, that boy, this boy, anyone.
He's lost his dignity; he's losing speed,
despite their chanted taunts to run! to run!
From someone's expert arm the treasure flies
just low enough to graze his fingertips,
too high to catch, but not to tantalize.
They laugh at how his belly, breasts, and hips
show quakes of jiggles as he turns around.

And on the outskirts, with a loser's art,
the second-fattest boy in school has found
a place to be a part but stand apart—
until a high and errant toss descends,
and in the small forever it will take
to fall to him he vaguely comprehends
the weighty choice that falls on him to make.[4]

---

4 "'Keepaway' is a close, canny observation of a situation I don't think I've ever before encountered in a poem."—Kelly Cherry, Final Judge, 2013 Able Muse Write Prize (for Poetry) on this third-place poem, "Keepaway," by Richard Wakefield.

Peter Svensson

A Photographic Exhibit

So . . . why photography?

Since forever I have been fascinated by three things: music, traveling and stories.

Stories: The stories my mother used to read to me when I was a child, the stories I later found reading books, the real stories I found watching other people's lives. And mine.

At some point I felt a strong urge to put on paper the words I had spinning round my head.

So I wrote.

Traveling: How would it be to go to this or that place? How do people live there? What kind of cultures, different ways of seeing life, would I find? I used to dream about it, I couldn't stay still. I had to go and find out. I had to see, to taste it.

So I went. And, remembering my first trip, I relive that mesmerizing feeling, that sudden awareness that the world "in fact existed."

Music: The sound, that beautiful sound, the first time I heard my mother playing the piano, still echoes in my mind. I was overwhelmed.

And the records my father listened to when I was a child. I was hypnotized.

I wanted to play. I had to play.

So I learned how to play.

And photography?

Well, somehow for me, photography—my photography, the way I see it, the way I feel it—came as a natural result of the many moments in my life I felt these three things coming together at once in my mind.

So I started taking photos.

How do these three main sources of inspiration come together in a photo? Well, I guess I must say that it's intuitive, and sometimes even against my will. . . .

Music. Every photo seems to have its own music, to flow to the sound of it. And many times a tune, even a particular song, pops out in my mind when I'm taking a photo. Or I feel I have to write a song about it.

Stories. To me, a photo always tells a story. A good photo at least. And I could write one story for every photo I take. It comes instantly to my mind when I'm shooting. Even when I think of how I'll shoot it.

Traveling. Any photo should be a journey on its own. Not a journey to the place it was taken, but to the atmosphere it carries, to the mood it embraces, to its own world.

And, most of all, a journey to our own feelings, to our own soul. And, therefore, also the feelings and the soul of the photographer.

For me, a really good photo should then, ideally, join together these three elements.

But, there is something, I think, that has to come as a result of this "ensemble"—most of all a good photo must induce the viewer to feel. Whatever the feeling might be. And it must be taken if the photographer feels it. As for myself, if I don't "feel" the photo, I simply don't take it. I'm not able to do it, in fact . . .

So, in the end, it all comes down to feelings and nothing else. Especially, it shouldn't have anything to do with what is used to take it, the technical resources. I personally don't care about the fabulous technology the photographer uses; I don't care about the remarkable definition of the picture. Neither do I care about the incredible amount of equipment sometimes involved in taking a photo. And I always stand at a complete loss about people who list all the "five hundred and twenty-four" items of technical equipment they use to take photos. It's as if you found next to Leonardo da Vinci's Mona Lisa, the list of brushes, paints and oils he used to paint it—"Hi! My name is Leonardo, and I used for painting the face a brush number 3.1 with a handle of 10.5 cm. . . ."

How much do I care about it? I don't. What does it matter?

No . . . the best photos are always the ones that simply hit you in your heart and soul and make you "feel." Even if sometimes you don't want to. That's what I care about. And those are the ones that can be taken with any kind of camera.

In fact, some of my favorite photos by other photographers actually have a terrible technical quality.

And some of my own favorite photos were taken with a very old cell-phone camera.

But they have their music, they make me travel, they tell me a story.

They make me feel.

★★★

Featured Art
FROM **PETER SVENSSON**

★ ★ ★

A LÉPCSŐN[5]

5 (The stairs)

Fragment

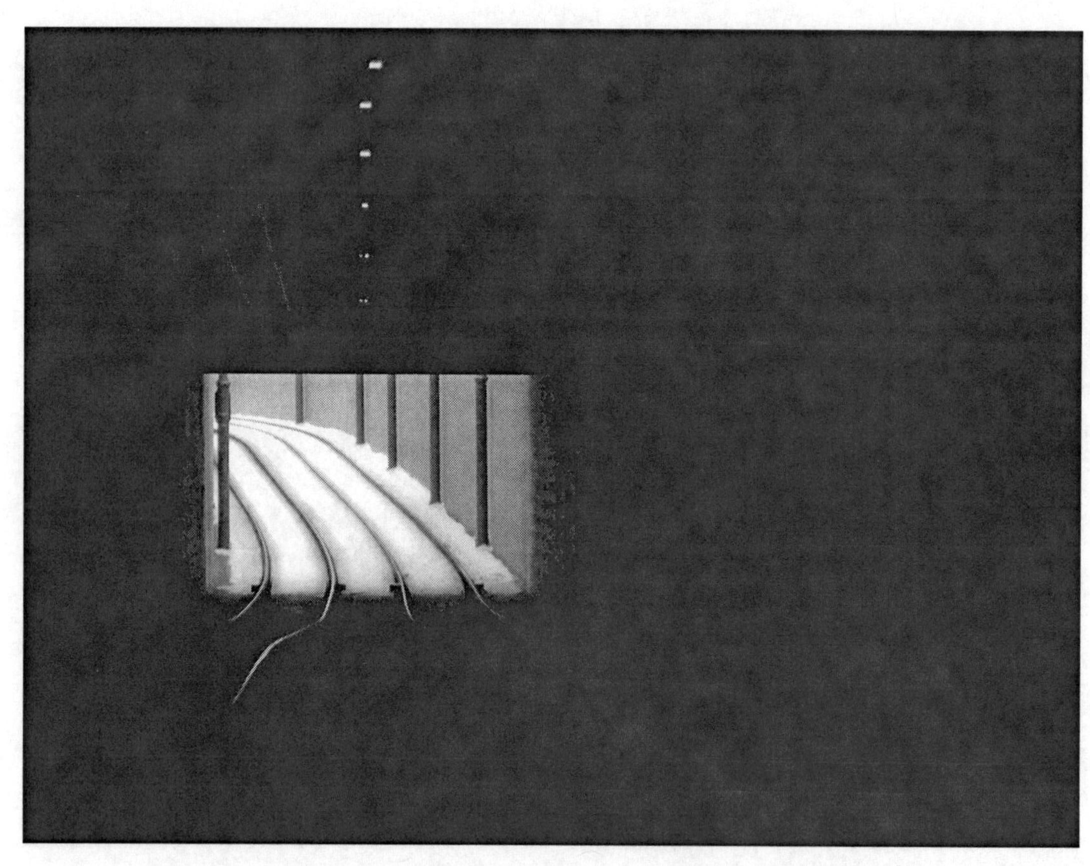

SINGLE TICKET, ROUNDTRIP, NO DISCOUNT . . .

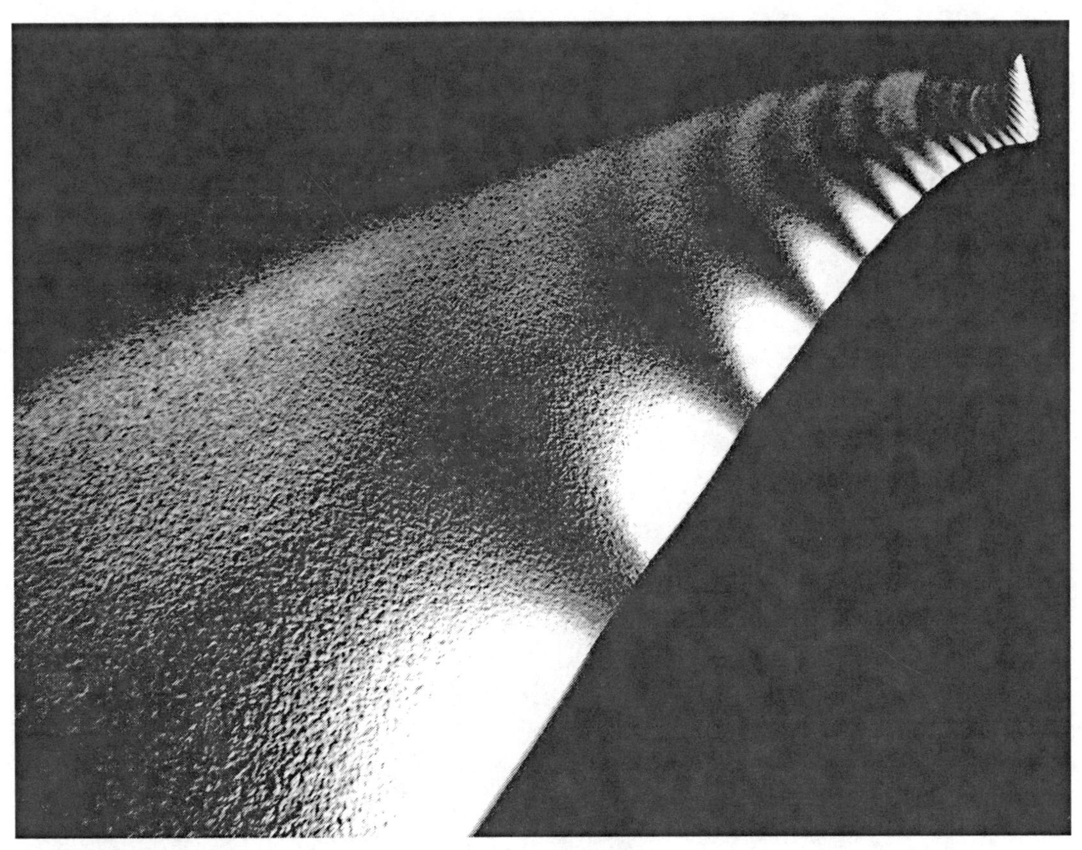

INTO

Красота[6]

6 (Beauty)

I'M SPINNING AROUND

JAZZ

PARADE

AND THEN ONE DAY YOU FIND, TEN YEARS BEHIND YOU, NO ONE TOLD YOU WHEN TO RUN, YOU MISSED THE STARTING GUN . . .[7]

7 Pink Floyd, "Time"

OLD FRIENDS

MOMENTS IN TIME

ПУТНИК[8]

8 (Wayfarer)

U-Bahn geschichten[9]

9 (Subway stories)

U-Bahn Geschichten 2[10]

10 (Subway stories 2)

THE COLD HAS A VOICE

THE HEART OF IT

Je vous regarde et je vois . . .[11]

11 (I look at you and I see . . .)

ESSAY

Peter Byrne

Pursuing Tennyson in Tight Shoes

Never—never more—oh, never
Did that Cricket leave him ever,
    Dawn or evening, day or night;
Clinging as a constant treasure,
Chirping with a cheerious measure,
Wholly to my uncle's pleasure
    (Though his shoes were far too tight).[1]

— "Some Incidents in the Life of My Uncle Arly" by Edward Lear

We come no more to that golden shore," murmured Edward Lear as he wrote the words in his diary, August 13, 1963.[2] At fifty-one he was back in England for a summer stay. To sell his artwork he had to mix socially with the upper classes. As always he had to deal with memories. That's where the line from Tennyson came in. Early on, Lear felt an affinity to Tennyson. "In Memoriam" recalled his own conviction that happiness existed only in the past and that beauty brought pain. The present had room for nothing but one long melancholic whine.

There was no remedy, only make-do stratagems. Detailing his sadness in diaries was one of them. Another was laborious travel and ceaseless work on his art. A third was writing and drawing Nonsense in which the whining became a funny mouse squeak. These were part of an overall strategy that Lear knew from the outset couldn't work. He sought perfect intimacy with someone, anyone, who was nice, all nice from tip to always male toe.

All this can be psychologized away by a neglected, shabby genteel childhood, an older sister's smothering love, hideous looks, clumsiness, bad eyesight, and epilepsy. But such consolation was not available to Lear at thirty-seven in 1849 when he made sure of failing in his search for a soul mate. He fixed on Frank Lushington, a close-mouthed, self-contained, indifferent prig. Lushington belonged to high society. Lear had come to frequent such people by a crooked route. He had been in their employ as an artist, taken their commissions, and entered their social life as an oddball *amuseur* who played, sang and concocted comic verse that he fitted with startling illustrations. He toadied with a will and had been called upon to give Queen Victoria drawing lessons. Left-handed prestige came to him as a published author and intrepid traveler.

Lushington's brother Henry had been a friend of Alfred Tennyson and Arthur Hallam at Cambridge. Tennyson used Hallam's early death to hold together the centrifugal parts of "In Memoriam." The poet's sister had married a Lushington and on a visit to their home he could not avoid meeting Frank's moonstruck hanger-on, "the dirty landscape painter," as Lear mocked himself. It was 1851 and Tennyson at forty had just lived his annus mirabilis. He had published "In Memoriam" and married Emily Sellwood. Both occasions were momentous. Lear had begun the poem seventeen years before and had been procrastinating about marrying Emily since 1936.

Lear relied on poetry, especially Tennyson's, for his vital balance. He followed up the introduction by one of his indirect approaches. He sent Emily two of his travel books. His covering letter said, "There have been few weeks or days within the last 8 years, that I have not been more or less in the habit of remembering or reading Tennyson's poetry, & the amount of pleasure derived by me from them has been quite beyond reckoning." Lear also mentioned for the first time in the 1851 letter a project that he would carry on until his death in 1888 and leave unfinished. "I intended long ago to have done a series of little landscapes illustrative of some of the poems, but a thousand things have stepped in between me & my wishes."

Lear's instinct had been sure and Emily replied warmly. She would not only be his conduit to the poet but his confidante, counseling him on his *peines d'amour*. They would gossip like a couple of matrons at a tea party. Tennyson's instinct about Emily had been no less sure. He married her after years of bookish passion with *femme-fatale* figures in his verse. Emily was the pragmatic solution whose role in life would be to magnify his glory, sit at home with his children and do his secretarial work. Since youth, Tennyson had been a past master at delegating power in everything that didn't concern writing poems. Lear's load of guilt kept him from acting similarly. He bewailed his responsibilities, but didn't refuse them though living abroad made them lighter. Here as so often he was the handsome

Tennyson's ugly twin, the loser in the winner's shadow.

Emily's qualifications for her marriage were a potential for self-sacrifice, plain looks and a religiosity shading to bigotry. Thomas Carlyle described her as "a freckly round-faced woman, rather tallish and without shape, a slight lisp too. . . ." Edmund Peel reported: "A very nice person, not handsome nor the reverse—and not with money nor absolutely without. . . ." As their married life progressed, Emily consolidated domestic power and refined her role. An acquaintance, Anne Gilchrist, found she gave too much importance to "position and appearances." As for her husband, "she surrounds him ever closer and closer with the sultry, perfumed atmosphere of luxury and homage in which his great soul—and indeed any soul would—droops and sickens." But Tennyson took pleasure in drooping and had always been on the sick side. Toward the end of his life, Lord Carnarvon noted of him, "He brings everything back to himself. His own writings are the central point of all his thoughts. . . . He hates the modern Radicals . . . and if he expresses an occasional belief in human or social progress it is a very frigid and doubtful profession of faith."

Emily was no challenge to Lear and could have been one of his older sisters with a larger vocabulary. Surprisingly, he overlooked her narrow piety, which ran contrary to his tolerant Christianity of simple decency and dislike of parsons and their sermons. Though he went on endlessly to her about Lushington's neglect of him, she preferred to ignore his passionate attraction to men. She even introduced him to a marriage prospect, a certain Miss Cotton whom in a blue funk he nixed out of hand. Lear and Emily became bosom correspondents in a friendship that puzzles. Lear needed sympathetic mother figures, but his praise for Emily got lost in the clouds of hyperbole. He claimed that she was equal to "fifteen angels, several hundreds of ordinary women, many philosophers" and much more.

For Tennyson, the initial contact proved the high point of his relationship with Lear. He read the *Albanian Journal* Lear sent and wrote the poem "To Edward Lear on His Travels in Greece," a hefty leg-up for the traveling artist.[3] Afterwards his only praise for Lear seems to have been for his performance of the poet's poems that Lear had set to music and sung while he played the piano. His lachrymose favorite, "Tears, Idle Tears," regularly served as an after-dinner digestive. The more musically minded, however, did not think much of Lear's "vamping" and humming along, attributing Tennyson's approval to his being no more of a musician than Lear.

Tennyson's ignoring of Lear was hardly a surprise. His undiluted attention to himself was constant from his penniless youth and Cambridge years through his laureateship and the House of Lords to his status as a national monument and death as an imperial figurehead. As he climbed in society he had little time for any but the illustrious, and to his credit even managed to snub some of them.

As an eccentric, likable but marginal, Lear was condescended to as he grew older, even by his good friends. His neediness came out strongly in his friendship with Emily, which was kept intimate through letters and visits. The Nonsense author beloved of children won over the Tennysons' two sons. However, the poet's coldness rankled and partly explains Lear's increasing strictures on Tennyson's behavior. He was distant and harsh to his sons and heaped too much work on Emily. The admirer spurned was talking, but his observations were exact.

Lear complained that on visits he never had a chance to talk to Tennyson alone. Hiking together the poet resorted to the tactic he also used when appearing in public. He maintained his solitude by reciting his own poems in a voice no one dared interrupt. When Lear lived in the country for a while with several Pre-Raphaelite painters, he invited Tennyson down for a "rural Sunday." The poet did not come.

Lear's lifelong inner debate, which he was given to dramatize at length for his acquaintances, concerned where he should live. It was a home or abroad dilemma that touched such matters as his age, health, career, childhood, bachelor status and, over all, his unfulfilled and surely unfulfillable longing. His attraction to the Tennysons comes out in a contorted proposal he made in a letter to Alfred in 1855:

"Do you think there is a Pharmouse or a Nin somewhere near you, where there would be a big room looking to the North?—so that I could paint in it quietly, & come and see you & Mrs Tennyson promiscuously? I know what you would say, or are saying—'come to us.' But that *wouldn't* do: the botherations of 6 feet paintings & all the combotherations of artists' ways *do not, & will not* dovetail with country houses in Anglosaxonland; I have tried the matter well—& know it to be so."

Like the rural Sunday, the offer was not taken up. Lear, however, would never manage to disentangle himself from the Tennysons. His wrong-side-up plan to illustrate the poet's lines with his own landscapes was another pact with failure. Rejigging it continually he resembled nothing so much as one of those distorted figures that illustrate his limericks. He would have to die to get free of the misshapen thing he created. That was of course the hidden logic of the operation. It kept him working to the end, giving him something to live for.

Landscape was not central to Tennyson's poetry. His aim was not to create Claude- or Turner-like scenes in words as Lear did with pen and paint on paper and canvas (with considerably less muscle than the masters). Tennyson did come up with some stunning descriptive phrases touching landscape. But he was interested in drama, which meant the doings of people. That they were versions of himself didn't lessen the theatricality. (He had wanted to call "In Memoriam" "The Way of the Soul," the soul being of course his soul. The other protagonist of the poem, energizing the author hero, was his mighty quatrain.)

What Lear found true in Tennyson's poetry was that happiness couldn't be repeated. But Tennyson's past happy moments took place with others. It would have been much more reasonable for Lear to illustrate Tennyson's poetry with depictions of the characters the poet created. Lear, however, was a landscape painter, and what had made him one was precisely his inability to deal with the human figure. He had been an ornithological draughtsman of extreme precision. But the human body was untouchable, perhaps out of disgust for his own and nervousness about the flesh of others. His project amounted to portraying a stage full of actors by an empty one, celebrating presence with absence.

In 1852 Lear wrote Emily saying he had made a list of "all the lines which convey to me in the most decided manner his [Tennyson's] genius for the perception of the beautiful in landscape." He explained that the poet's descriptions of certain places were as accurate as if he had used them as models. But it would have taken more than genius for Tennyson to reproduce like a camera what he had never seen. Lear was foisting his own criteria on Tennyson. He was a landscape painter who in his own estimation achieved "good Topographical likenesses" with poetic touches. He drew real places: "The peculiarity of my work lies, I believe, in its accuracy. . . ." Lear here took his misconception a step further. The lines he extracted did not represent the poem they were taken from but were simply plucked for their topographical incisiveness.

Tennyson was someone for whom the phrase "couldn't have cared less" was invented. He'd read Lear's gift book, written a poem about it and was finished with him. As William Gaunt tells us in *The Pre-Raphaelite Dream,* Tennyson's "indifference to the visual arts was entire." He did not care about being illustrated, considering it a theft of his thunder. He even found fault with the famous illustrated Moxon edition of his poems of 1857 with work by W.G. Rossetti, John Everett Millais and Holman Hunt. He said what he had to say in words and saw illustrations as superfluous if not downright adversarial. Tennyson was no paltry egoist who thought that any attention to himself could be useful. He was a megalomaniac who thought no reference to himself could ever be adequate.

Lear's approach to Tennyson took the form of a scheme Tennyson didn't care about, proposed by a man whom he kept at a distance. In this situation Lear turned to Emily to keep the Tennyson connection alive. His adulation of her looked like a way of getting back at Tennyson for his indifference and of still remaining in the poet's orbit.

As Lear's dislike of Tennyson the man increased, so did his dislike of his later poetry, which he found a rerun of earlier work. Still, he never backed off the illustration project. Travel and other work had got in the way, but he regularly shuffled his plan and earmarked landscapes for it. When in 1870 he finally settled in his own house in San Remo, he intended to engage with it in earnest. Once his trip to India was out of the way, he plunged in and began five large oil paintings on Tennysonian subjects. Lear was never at ease in oil but at the time his natural gift as a watercolorist was not well rewarded. Large oils, landmark pictures like the ones the Pre-Raphaelites were turning out, could be very profitable.

In 1881 he moved to what he christened Villa Tennyson, his second San Remo house, and felt, at sixty-nine, it was now or never. He wrote Holman Hunt that he was beginning a new group of three hundred Tennyson drawings: "in their final or Butterfly Condition. For at Clive Farm [in 1852] they were in the Egg State: & next I advanced them to a larger size which may be called their Caterpillar Life. Then came detailed monochrome outlines of the full size they are to be, & that is their Chrysalis Condition—whence the next move is the last & present one."

When he turned to smaller formats that could go into books, the impossibility of his scheme came home to him. Color was out of the question for small drawings and he went on to monochrome. But it was reproducing his work that presented an unsolvable problem. The methods available—autotype, lithography, engraving, etching, photography, platinotype, aquatint, he tried them all—were either incapable of rendering a picture's delicacy or so expensive as to make a book unsalable.

In 1885, in a rush forward to flee such problems, he wrote a four-hundred-word dedication to Lady Tennyson for a publication that would never exist, *Landscape Illustrations of Poems by Lord Tennyson.* It was a scaled-down version of his dream but hinted at much more to come. Ten drawings of the two hundred finished would be published "to be more or less prolonged according to its success."

In the dedication Lear innocently underlines what a hodgepodge he has in mind: "The subjects are not equally connected with, or parallel to the quotations they illustrate: some being simply literal portraits (as Cannes, Mar Sabbas &c.), while others (as the Lotos Eaters, Enoch Arden &c.), although mostly drawn from real scenes are by no means to be looked on as correct Topographical likenesses. Again, other subjects represent scenes widely separated from the places described in the poems, though in full accord with the quotations, such as 'the sun fell & all the land was dark,' 'Rosy blossom in hot ravine'—&c., &c. In general, only one or two subjects have been taken from a poem."

Lear closes the fantasy dedication: "I may well leave this world with a satisfaction I might not have attained to, had I not resolved to make & to publish this Collection of Poetical Topographical Tennysoniana."

In May 1887 he was still trying to interest publishers. The following January he did in fact leave the world. He had made the Collection, indeed made and unmade it more than once, in half a dozen different, unfinished forms. But nothing was published until 1889 when one hundred copies of a small book appeared containing three of Tennyson's poems and a few of Lear's illustrations.[4]

It remained for Ruth Pitman's *Edward Lear's Tennyson,* a century later in 1988, to spread before us various surviving elements of Lear's scheme. She reproduces one of the two surviving sets of two hundred designs. These are the "Eggs," roughly 4 x 6 inches, that Lear wrote about to Holman Hunt in 1881. She accompanies many of them with part or all of the Tennyson poem that Lear thought corresponded to his drawing, adding quotes from Lear about its composition and her own commentary on the connection between each poem and drawing. Pitman's admiration for Lear doesn't lead her to overlook the oddity of the whole undertaking: "Lear avoided depicting Tennyson's characters and their interactions completely. He chose a line, or several, describing landscape and delved into his own journeys for an illustration that might relate to that line, but not necessarily to the rest of the poem." It was inevitable perhaps that Pitman's eminently useful book pays homage to Lear by suggesting in its organization the Rube Goldberg nature of his project. Let us pluck several Eggs from her basket and see how they stand up to her conclusion.

"Egg" number 1 is "Mariana" from *Poems, Chiefly Lyrical 1830*. Each of its seven stanzas ends with the refrain which fixes the mood inexorably: "She said [or wept], 'I am aweary, aweary,/ I would that I were dead!'" Now Lear in his diary would repeat, sometimes with irony but often in moments of loneliness, "I am aweary, aweary." He clearly understood and felt the poem but took a step backward from it. The line he chose to illustrate, as always writing it beneath the drawing, was "the day/ Was sloping toward his western bower." He selected four of his landscapes to represent it. They were all sunsets, one at Cannes in France, another at Albenga in Italy and two from the vicinity of Bombay in India.

"Eggs" 50, 51, 52 and 53 refer to the "The Lotos-Eaters" whose Spenserian lines lap on like eternal surf. Lear is impressed enough to choose four separate particles to illustrate: "A land of streams"; "They sat them down upon the yellow sand"; "still waters between walls/ Of shadowy granite, in a gleaming pass"; and "To watch the crisping ripples on the beach/ And tender curving lines of creamy spray." Rare for him, he includes some minute human figures. They are blobs and splashes strewn uncomfortably on the doubtless incandescent sand. The artist who in old age still winced over the masturbations of his childhood wasn't going to set up a Homeric debauch. Instead we get a huge load of rock and water from Macedonia, Greece, Egypt and Albania.

Turning pages quickly in search of something like action, we pull up at "Eggs" 195 and 199, devoted to the Guinevere section of *The Idylls of the King* that Tennyson simmered over for fifty years. Surely a fallen woman full of guilty eloquence would pry Lear's eyes from mountain tops.

> "O Lancelot, if thou love me get thee hence."
> And then they were agreed upon a night
> (When the good King should not be there) to meet
> And part for ever. Passion-pale they met
> And greeted: hands in hands, and eye to eye,
> Low on the border of her couch they sat
> Stammering and staring: it was their last hour,
> A madness of farewells.

Lear shows no perturbation. The lines he excerpts are "Between the steep cliff and the coming sea" and "On some vast plain before a setting sun." We are treated to a view of Beachy Head's white cliffs of Sussex, and a sunset over Thebes in Egypt.

The Lear mystery isn't about what we don't know of his personal life. His surviving diaries tell us more than we want to know. His epileptic seizures are carefully counted, his moments of boredom and loneliness lamented endlessly. Among his flow of doubts, there are even some moments of joy recalled. But what remains impenetrable is the connection between his sober depictions of landscape and his vein of preposterous Nonsense. Hidden gleams of "seriousness" can be caught sight of in his great poems. The Tennysonian music and pathos show through the rough knit of desperate laughter. The Pelican Chorus sings:

> And far away in the twilight sky,
> We heard them singing a lessening cry,
> Farther and farther till out of sight,
> And we stood alone in the silent night!
> Often since, in the nights of June,
> We sit on the sand and watch the moon;
> She has gone to the great Gromboolian plain,
> And we will probably never meet again!

We can almost speak of a parody by a diffident and too respectful admirer. Listen to the Dong with a Luminous Nose:

> And now each night, and all night long,
> Over those plains still roams the Dong;
> And above the wail of Chimp and Snipe
> You may hear the squeak of his plaintive pipe
> While ever he seeks, but seeks in vain
> To meet with his Jumbly girl again,
> Lonely and wild—all night he goes—
> The Dong with a luminous Nose!

Lear, however, is most identified with limericks.[5] Interpretation has to be pushed hard to find anything nineteenth-century "serious" in them. Emotion is not welcome and treated roughly. And what seriousness could stand up to his accompanying illustrations? A typical Lear limerick reads:

> There was an Old Man at a Station,
> Who made a promiscuous Oration;
> But they said, "Take some snuff!—

You have talk'd quite enough,
You afflicting Old Man at a Station!"

This is closer to childhood than a "modern" limerick like this one of Conrad Aiken:

It's time to make love, douse the glim;
The fireflies twinkle and dim;
The stars lean together
Like birds of a feather,
And the loin lies down with the limb.

Lear never aimed at a witty punch line. (He left the rational approach to Lewis Carroll.) He didn't resort to tricky internal rhymes or a steady flow of verbal high jinks. His limericks generally fade out in a sigh-like near repetition of their initial line. Despite all his travel, he was trapped in stasis, ever-repeated impotent desire. For forty years he yearned to enter Tennyson's world, all the time knowing he would never make the leap.

There was an old man whose look
Kept him aloft like a rook
When a bee in his bonnet
Rubbed his nose in a sonnet
He came down to aw shucks and ah shoot!

★★★

Notes

1.

Editor's Note: The punctuation in this and the other quoted poems in this essay have been modernized to improve readability.

2.

The essential books on the subject are Noakes' and Pitman's. Bachelor's is a useful recent biography of Tennyson. There are various editions of Lear's correspondence. On Lear, Marco Graziosi's nonsenselit.org is an invaluable source of information and even of his never-published material.

Noakes, Vivien: *Edward Lear, The Life of a Wanderer,* Ariel Books BBC, 1968, revised 1988, 304 pages.

Edward Lear's Tennyson, with an introduction and commentaries by Ruth Pitman, extensively illustrated, Carcanet, 1988, 215 pages.

Batchelor, John: *Tennyson: To Strive, to Seek, to Find,* Chatto & Windus, 2012, 448 pages.

3.

To Edward Lear on His Travels in Greece

Illyrian woodlands, echoing falls
Of water, sheets of summer glass,
The long divine Peneian pass,
The vast Akrokeraunian walls,
Tomohrit, Athos, all things fair,
With such a pencil, such a pen,
You shadow forth to distant men,
I read and felt that I was there:
And trust me while I turn'd the page,
And track'd you still on classic ground,
I grew in gladness till I found
My spirits in the golden age.
For me the torrent ever pour'd
And glisten'd—here and there alone
The broad-limb'd gods at random thrown
By fountain urns; and Naiads oar'd
A glimmering shoulder under gloom
Of cavern pillars; on the swell
The silver lily heaved and fell;
And many a slope was rich in bloom
From him that on the mountain lea
By dancing rivulets fed his flocks,
To him who sat upon the rocks,
And fluted to the morning sea.

Twenty years later in a letter of 28 February, 1872, Lear would fashion a mnemonic that was also a parody of the first eight lines of "To Edward Lear."

Delirious Bulldogs; echoing calls
My daughter, green as summer grass;
The long supine Plebeian ass,
The nasty crockery boring falls;
Tom-Moory Pathos; all things bare,
With such a turket! such a hen!
And scrambling forms of distant men,
O! ain't you glad you were not there!

4.

Poems of Alfred, Lord Tennyson. Illustrated by Edward Lear. Boussod, Valadon & Co., 1889.

5.

A limerick has five lines rhymed a-a-b-b-a, its first, second and fifth lines contain three feet (usually an iamb and two anapests), while its third and fourth lines contain two beats (usually two anapests).

Jehanne Dubrow

Interviewed by Anna M. Evans

Jehanne Dubrow is the author of four poetry collections, including most recently *Red Army Red* and *Stateside* (Northwestern University Press, 2012 and 2010). Her first book, *The Hardship Post* (2009), won the Three Candles Press Open Book Award, and her second collection, *From the Fever-World,* won the Washington Writers' Publishing House Poetry Competition (2009). She has been a recipient of the Alice Fay Di Castagnola Award from the Poetry Society of America, the Towson University Prize for Literature, an Individual Artist's Award from the Maryland State Arts Council, a Walter E. Dakin Fellowship and Howard Nemerov Poetry Scholarship from the Sewanee Writers' Conference, and a Sosland Foundation Fellowship from the Center for Advanced Holocaust Studies at the U.S. Holocaust Memorial Museum. Her poetry, creative nonfiction, and book reviews have appeared in *The New Republic, Poetry, Ploughshares, The Hudson Review, Prairie Schooner, American Life in Poetry,* and on *Poetry Daily* and *Verse Daily.* She serves as the Director of the Rose O'Neill Literary House and is an assistant professor in creative writing at Washington College, on the Eastern Shore of Maryland.

◊ ◊ ◊ ◊

AME: You have published four books in four years, which makes you either very talented or very lucky—probably both! What advice would you give to those of us, like myself, who are stalled at that often-repeated finalist/semi-finalist stage?

JD: So much of publication comes down to luck. But, in my experience, not every manuscript is right for a book competition; sometimes really excellent poetry collections are likelier to find homes when they're sent to open submission periods instead. Contests often seem to favor really loud—or what I think of as voice-driven—manuscripts, so that a quieter, more meditative book may have a difficult time being heard. It's important to know the "volume" of your poems and to recognize what this means for your manuscript when it's read blind, when it's one of many in a large stack of anonymous collections.

AME: Your identity as a Jewish poet is central to two of your collections, *The Hardship Post* and *From the Fever-World,* but takes a back seat in *Stateside* and *Red Army Red.* You also wrote an essay for the Mezzo Cammin Women Poet's Timeline on Emma Lazarus and her struggle with the "tension between citizenship and cultural identity." What does being a "hyphenated writer" mean to you?

JD: I see the problem of identity as central to all my work. As you say, in *The Hardship Post* and *From the Fever-World,* it's Jewishness that I'm picking apart, trying to figure out what it means, respectively, to be an American Jew in a post-Holocaust landscape or a feminist in a world of Orthodox Judaism.

In *Stateside,* I ask how one maintains a separate, distinct self while being "married to the military." The military wife is expected to remain fixed and unchanging, while her husband has movement and agency; the poems in *Stateside* challenge that very restrictive model.

Red Army Red is a book about girlhood. Because I came of age in Poland, during the final years of the Eastern Bloc, I use the oppressive language of Communism to speak about the oppressiveness of the adolescent body. *Red Army Red* considers the intersection between personal and public identity, between the body and the body politic. I'm always looking for that push-pull, those interesting moments of tension, which shape our identities and make all of us hyphenated creatures.

AME: You and I are of similar ages, so I recall the events in Poland from the perspective of what was happening in the UK at the time. It's fascinating to me that your father actually met Lech Wałęsa! Some moments and places in time embody the spirit of an era, and in *Red Army Red,* you have captured much of that. To what extent do you believe poets should seek out such moments and places and make it our job to put them on record?

JD: I like the idea that poets—that writers, that artists in general—have a responsibility in what they choose to represent. There's that iconic moment in Anna Akhmatova's "Requiem." The poet-speaker, who is waiting in a line outside Leningrad prison, is asked by another woman, "can anyone ever describe this," *this* being atrocity, loss, and history.

The speaker answers, "I can." And Czesław Miłosz's "Dedication" asks "what is poetry which does not save/ Nations or people?"

During my years behind the Iron Curtain, I learned from the Polish artists that their duty was to record. They painted or wrote or composed as a way of documenting Soviet rule. And, most tellingly, as Communism in Eastern Europe began to crumble, they expressed fears about what would happen to their art. What would their work mean once there was no longer an oppression to push against?

AME: How do you feel about the fact that the Holocaust is an inevitable subject for a Jewish poet?

JD: I'm not sure that the Holocaust is an inevitable subject for all Jewish poets. It was, however, inevitable for me. My parents are first-generation Americans, Ashkenazi Jews whose families fled Central and Eastern Europe in the late 1930s, coming to the United States and to Latin America. Both of my parents grew up in German-speaking households, and the Shoah was always either a shadow or a felt presence. As far back as I can remember, my mother's mother—my Oma—told me stories about those final days in Germany. Her stories were usually close-calls or disasters that turned out to be life-saving moments in disguise. For instance, her whole family once came down with food poisoning. It was Passover, and the main course (fish) turned out to be spoiled. Her father died from the meal, after the hospital refused to admit a Jew for care. The day after her father's burial, the Gestapo showed up, looking for him. My great-grandmother said, "I'll take you to him." She walked them to the cemetery, pointed at the new grave, and said, "You want him? There he is." Within a week, the family decided they had to leave and managed to get visas to Honduras *just in time*.

I spent seven years of my childhood and adolescence in Poland. I loved Warsaw. I loved speaking Polish. I loved the Poles who taught me and took care of me and, in many cases, helped to raise me. Like other American Jews, I should have hated Poland and believed that Poles were "worse than the Germans" (this is an important trope in many Holocaust narratives). So, it was inevitable that I use poetry to sort through my complex feelings about a place that I had experienced so intimately.

AME: When you mention Poland, Wisława Symborska and Anna Swir immediately come to my mind. Both have been translated of course, but is translation something you have ever undertaken? Or are you content with your ability to read them in the original?

JD: I've translated from the French and the Polish (a hodgepodge: Mickiewicz, Herbert, Baudelaire, Prévert). But I've never undertaken a really serious or extended translation project. It's on my to-do list, along with writing a stage play, collaborating on a musical or an opera, and venturing into short or flash fiction.

AME: *From the Fever-World* is written in the voice of an imaginary turn-of-the-century Yiddish poet called Ida, sent to you as a ghost by your grandmothers, as the dedication states. Were you attempting to give your grandmothers a voice, with these poems? Did either of them know you as a poet, and how do you think they might have reacted to this book?

JD: One of my grandmothers died when I was seven years old and the other when I was a junior in college. They never knew me as poet. But I inherited, from both of them, my talent for sewing and other kinds of needlework. My Oma was trained in haute couture; I believe that, were it not for the war, we would know her name today as an important figure in high fashion.

When I wrote *From the Fever-World,* I kept asking "what if?" What if a brilliant, imaginative, restless woman tried to write subversive, experimental poems while living in a tiny town in southern Poland during the interwar period? What if Ida Lewin, an Orthodox Jew with access to little education, still found a way to stitch tiny, beautiful words out of the tedium of women's work? I don't remember my father's mother very well, but I think my Oma would be fiercely proud of the life I've made for myself, both off the page and on it.

AME: I think she would be too! Have sewing or needlework ever featured in any of your poems? I feel as if they could provide a storehouse of metaphorical materials!

JD: I've thought a lot about my grandmothers' needlework in drafting my most recently completed collection, *The Arranged Marriage,* a book of prose poems about my mother's strange, Jewish-Latina upbringing in Honduras and El Salvador. My Oma—with her gifts as a designer/seamstress/businesswoman—is one of the brave or heroic figures in the collection.

AME: *From the Fever-World* also contains a number of poems for which you have provided several versions, a trick that reminded me of Robert Lowell revisiting his sonnets. Did you have Lowell in mind, or was this simply a way of enhancing the verisimilitude of Ida? If not Lowell, who would you cite as influences?

JD: In writing *From the Fever-World,* I was really influenced by a wonderful anthology called *The Imaginary Poets,* edited by Alan Michael Parker. Every contributor to the book invented his or her own poet-persona, each one with a rich backstory and an aesthetic rooted in history and place. I wanted Ida Lewin to be as real and convincing a poet as I could make her. I wanted her to second-guess her own choices—the way all writers do—writing multiple versions of her poems, as a natural part of the drafting process. And because Ida's poems weren't "published" but found buried in a box, long after her death by influenza, it seemed only natural to me that she might have left behind competing drafts of many of her poems.

AME: Alan Michael Parker is a fantastic poet and a personal friend of mine from VCCA[1]. Is that where you met him? Four books in four years also seems extraordinary from the perspective of the sheer volume of work required, and I know you have been a full-time faculty member throughout this period too. Were you at any artists' residencies, on sabbatical at all, or are you just a prolific writer?

JD: You know what's funny? I've only met Alan Michael Parker once or twice at the annual AWP[2] Conference; it's interesting how, so often, our mentors are people we only know from their powerful presence on the page.

I've only had one residency: a glorious and extremely productive month at the VCCA. But, I find that gatherings like the AWP Conference, the West Chester Poetry Conference, and the Sewanee Writers' Conference are a meaningful way to stay connected to our small tribe of poets.

It's true that I am very prolific. I write every day. In order to avoid boring myself, I work on several books at one time. Right now, I'm in the process of drafting two new books of poems, *Stories of the Great Operas* and *The Long Deployment.* I am also writing "meditative close readings" of poems by Philip Larkin, which will eventually become a collection of essays (if all goes well, that is).

AME: *Stateside,* which is focused on the experience of being a military wife whose husband has been deployed, is possibly your collection containing the most poems with a definite allegiance to form. What do you see as the relationship between form and subject, and why did this subject lend itself especially to rhyme? Do you approach writing in free verse and in form differently or in the same way?

JD: I see *The Hardship Post, Stateside,* and *Red Army Red* as being equally attached to fixed and received forms. But, *Stateside* is the most overt in its handling of form, probably because military life is itself so very formal. When soldiers march, that's a rhyming of bodies. A room full of officers in uniform is a visual rhyme. Because *Stateside* is an emotionally

1 Virginia Center for the Creative Arts
2 Association of Writers & Writing Programs

charged book, I often found the restrictive, protective shape of a form such as the sonnet especially useful when writing about the containment of fears and anxieties associated with military marriages.

As we know, free verse has its own rules, conventions, and formal constraints. For example, when I'm working in free verse, I often use the right-hand margin to determine a line length for the poem as a whole, which will then shape the poem's metrical patterns, its syntax, its diction, even its rhetoric. Working in free verse requires the poet to make decisions about form; when we work in fixed forms, many of those decisions have already been made for us.

The point is to remain open-minded. What form is suggested by subject matter? Sometimes, I'm drafting and I realize that this poem *must* become a villanelle. Perhaps, its preoccupation with a repeating event demands the villanelle's interwoven music, its obsessive refrains. On the other hand, sometimes a draft takes a really long time to tell me what form it wants to take. I've read that Zuni carvers believe the shape of the animal is embedded inside the stone; it's the task of the carver to work patiently until the form of the fetish reveals itself.

AME: I agree with you about villanelles! I even have the same feeling about sestinas, but the form I inevitably fall back on is the sonnet. Fourteen lines just seems to be the perfect length for many of the ideas I'm trying to explore. Most of your poems are also shorter narrative-lyrics. Can you see yourself ever writing a long narrative poem, like Mason's *Ludlow?* In fact, how is your next book taking shape?

JD: The sonnet is my default setting too! I just adore the argument and the music of those fourteen lines. But, I'm really interested in longer narrative forms, in part because an effective music becomes more difficult to sustain. And I like difficulty.

One of my current projects is a book of poems about my father's love of opera, *Stories of the Great Operas.* Because opera itself is expansive and plot-based, I now have an excuse (an excuse rooted in the relationship between form and content) to practice writing longer poems that focus on storytelling and on the construction of narrative. And, the book that I recently finished, *The Arranged Marriage,* treats the prose poem as a chapter in miniature, each poem functioning like a tiny piece of novel.

AME: Your childhood as the daughter of diplomats in Poland during the Cold War provided you with the material for *Red Army Red.* What other effects did it have on you as a writer?

JD: I grew up all over the world. I was born in Italy and lived in Yugoslavia, Zaire, Poland, Belgium, and Austria, occasionally returning to the United States throughout my childhood.

My parents both speak seven languages. When we lived abroad, we were always the kind of diplomatic family that focused on immersion rather than on trying to create some kind of "temporary America." So, I see myself as an American poet whose perspective remains international, whose work is consistently defined by a personal engagement with history, because I lived in places where big histories were happening and the experience was made personal for me.

AME: I think that's why your poetry resonates with so many people. *Stateside* has seven reviews on Amazon, and they don't all appear to be by people who know you—which I fear is the norm for contemporary poetry books. It's been a pleasure to talk with you, and I think your future holds great honors.

JD: Thank you, Anna! It's such an honor to be able to speak about the quiet work that we do and to know that someone is reading.

Jehanne Dubrow

Age Ten

— D. 328/Op. 1, Franz Schubert

When I'm bad, my father likes to sing
the opening bars of "The Erlking."
All night I lie awake and hear
the sound of hoof beats coming near—
the triple notes that make me cling

to my teddy bear (I'm crying).
All night the willow branches swing
against the hollow of my ear.
When I am bad,

the mist becomes a silver ring,
an ever-tightening wisp of string.
I tell it, *Go, just disappear.*
All night I tell myself that fear
is light—it's not a solid thing,
when I am bad.

Jehanne Dubrow

Overture

The velvet hinge becomes a velvet seat.
The program tells a story so grim
you're grateful for the orchestra—a gap

between audience and stage. You clap
before the curtain opens on a scrim
painted to look like a palace. You beat

the time signature on your armrest.
The important themes are here—a king's
insistent bass, a wife turned cello,

the thin whine of the violin you know
to be a daughter. The scrape of strings
is human voices speaking—how what's suppressed

will sing, how opera collapses and floats
because you can't, how all the instruments
will find a place inside the pit of you.

And in the dark, you lean—not toward the view
which can't be seen—but to the dissonance,
the tiny, clustered families made of notes.

Jehanne Dubrow

Ghazal for the Lost Operas

The adman pitches cheap cologne on stage.
He guzzles scotch, answers the phone on stage.

A city burns. And though the angels warn
of it, a wife turns salty stone on stage.

The alleyway is rat and flea and dog-
eat-dog, each fighting for a bone on stage.

Call her a lady of reclining night.
There's little that she hasn't blown on stage.

Beneath the white clematis, clinging vines,
they find a Giant overgrown on stage.

Miss Scarlet's dead by candlestick inside
the study. The killer isn't shown on stage.

The thread conspires against the needle,
all knotted up at being sewn on stage.

By day he's millionaire, by night a masked
crusader, right-hooking crime alone on stage.

No plot tonight. But only naked rows
of notes, and every act twelve-tone on stage.

When I was twelve, the dust-motes flickered gold.
Years flicker by—now I'm Saint Joan on stage.

Jehanne Dubrow

Figaro Redoublé

The Count loves anyone who's not
  his wife—the serving girl, the maid,
the pink-cheeked cook. It seems he's hot
  for every bosom in brocade,

each lacy ankle and loosened braid.
  He'll bribe. Some ladies can be bought.
He'll beg if it will get him laid.
  The Count loves anyone who's not

called consort, partner, spouse. A lot
  of men agree—who hasn't strayed?
Who hasn't (once or twice) forgot
  his wife? The serving girl, the maid—

hard to resist this damp parade
  of women on their knees. They squat
or bend. And he has gladly splayed
  the pink-cheeked cook. It seems he's hot

for wench and nanny. He wants a shot
  at every chamois cloth, the suede
of them, the box, the velvet spot.
  For every bosom in brocade

there is a hand. In masquerade,
    the feather duster's quickly caught,
the scepter seldom disobeyed.
    Come here, he says, Untie that knot—
        I can love anyone.

Jehanne Dubrow

What My Father Loves

More than anything, he loves the trills,
the sleek, gymnastic leap and run:
the coloratura of Beverly Sills.

Her voice has legs. It climbs the hills,
wears wings of wax and flies to the sun.
More than anything, he loves the trills,

the caramel, the fondant frills
of her. She's candy, sugar-spun.
The coloratura of Beverly Sills

has presence and body, how it fills
a room, how it weighs a ton
more than anything. He loves the trills

in their shattering. Everyone stills,
coffee unpoured, laundry undone.
The coloratura of Beverly Sills

is heat against glass. It distills
the world to itself—itself the one.
More than anything, he loves the trills.
The coloratura. Beverly Sills.

A.E. Stallings

Hecht's Brazen Recasting of Horace

I first encountered the work of Anthony Hecht with *The Venetian Vespers,* which I picked up at a bookstore as much for the look of it as anything. It was beautiful, rather austerely narrow and tall, with a distinctive fuchsia dust jacket and line drawings of Venice over a pale green cloth cover. I treasured it as an object even before I had come to appreciate the poetry.

It was not an easy book to enter. Certainly I was attracted to the shapely and rhythmic lines—in those days, in the early 1990s, when I knew little of what was going on in contemporary poetry, just to encounter a book in which there was meter and rhyme was revelatory. *The Venetian Vespers* begins with a number of long narrative poems in blank verse, displaying an Old World urbanity that made me feel callow. I found myself drawn toward the middle of the book, with its shorter and often rhymed lyrics, to get my footing.

It was with a jolt of recognition and delight that I came across "Application for a Grant." Horace's Odes were something I felt I *did* have a handle on—I recognized the Ode 1.1 in spite of its contemporary makeover before seeing "freely from Horace" at the bottom of the page—and so I felt I was able to enter this on terms of equality, at least as a reader and scholar. My study of the Latin poets was at the nexus of my poetic self—I felt that those ancient poems, for all that they were in dead languages and elaborate meters, were more modern, more contemporary, and spoke to me more directly than most of what I was reading in magazines. But this was something I only felt reading the original, not translations, which often exhaled the chalk dust of the 19th-century classroom. Encountering this playful but not trivializing verse version by Hecht had an immediate and lasting effect on me as both a poet and translator—in one stroke it seemed to grant permission to take wider liberties than I had thought possible, the sort of liberties that are rooted in a deep intimacy—a vigorous engagement and dialogue with the original without pedantic deference (no coughing in ink here). Horace begins:

> Maecenas atavis edite regibus,
> o et praesidium et dulce decus meus,
> sunt quos curriculo pulverem Olympicum
> collegisse iuvat metaque fervidis
> evitata rotis palmaque nobilis
> terrarum dominos evehit ad deos. . . .

> [O Maecenas, sprung of kingly forebears, my fortress and my sweet honor, there are those who rejoice to gather Olympic dust with their chariots—their blazing wheels having cleared the turning point, they are exalted by the famed palm of victory from earthly lords to the level of gods. . . .]

T.E. Page in his commentary encapsulates the poem economically: "Many and various are the pursuits and aims of men to which they cling tenaciously, glory, wealth, ease, war, sport; I, with the help of heaven, long to be a lyric poet, and if you, Maecenas, consider me one, I shall have attained the height of my ambition."

It has been suggested convincingly by C.W. Nauck, editor of the 1894 Teubner edition, that the first two lines and the last two were tacked on as an afterthought to an already completed poem, but as the poem stands we have both a graceful dedication and an announcement of lyric ambition intertwined. This priamel device—a preamble that sets up a foil for a contrasting statement—"some men desire this, others this; but as for me"—reminds us of Sappho's famous lines:

> Some there are who say that the fairest thing seen
> on the black earth is an array of horsemen;
> some, men marching; some would say ships; but I say
> she whom one loves best
>
> (trans. Richard Lattimore)

Part of the charm of Sappho's construction is the way in which she balances public and martial matters against something as private as lyric longing. Horace's catalogue will likewise play with proportions and expectations—the Olympic athlete against the seeker of high office, the soldier versus the farmer and merchant, the winebibber versus the hunter. No mention is made of love, an expectation we might have carried over from Sappho, save perhaps its implication in the blushing bride forgotten by a husband once his hunting-dog is on the scent. And what is it that Horace himself desires? Not much, it turns out—only the poet's ivy and a place among the immortal lyric poets. He undercuts this ambition in a typically Horatian way—*if* the Muses don't disallow it—and anyway if *you* consider me one, it will be enough. It's a graceful and charming compliment, but we don't really buy it—Horace is clearly aiming for the stars. The real compliment is that he is going to immortalize Maecenas by attaching his name to a great book.

Patronage of today's poets of course is handled by universities, foundations, and endowments. Hecht brilliantly lambastes this culture by simply updating 1.1 as, of course, a grant application. Hecht begins:

> Noble executors of the munificent testament
> Of the late John Simon Guggenheim, distinguished bunch
> Of benefactors, there are certain kinds of men
> Who set their hearts on being bartenders,
> For whom a life upon duck-boards, among fifths,
> Tapped kegs and lemon twists, crowded with lushes
> Who can master neither their bladders nor consonants,
> Is the only life, greatly to be desired.

Well, we've come down a bit from patrons descended from Etruscan kings! I love the control of registers of diction here, and registers of *syntax*, if I may say that. One sees mixed registers all the time nowadays—it is a tic of Ashbery's epigonoi—but done so consistently and to such little purpose it is more like a twelve-tone method to prevent any one key's dominant chord. Latinate vocabulary ("munificent testament") as heavy and dark as furniture at the law-firm of Serious, Sombre, and Grimm, suddenly gives way to the distinguished "bunch" of benefactors, and we know (as of course we were expecting from the title) that the seriousness is mock-seriousness. Hecht's first example, far from being Olympic glory, is aspiring bartenders, another sharp undercutting that allows him to relish another world of words—duck-boards, fifths, tapped kegs, lushes—and there's a suggestion of a pun here—the drunk might pronounce "incontinent" as "inconsonant"—all archly slotted into a Latinate syntax that ends on the translator's hoary "greatly to be desired."

But Hecht keeps the original Horatian catalogue in his sights even when he departs from it: the politician seeking the triple honors is suddenly and sinisterly the man who seeks "the White House, there to compose/ Rhythmical lists of enemies". And just when you think Hecht has dropped all notion of those opening Olympic charioteers, he gets them in with a sly wink of an idiom (italics mine):

Nothing could bribe your Timon, your charter member
Of the Fraternal Order of Grizzly Bears to love
His fellow, whereas it's just the opposite
With interior decorators; *that's what makes horse races.*

(Timon is Hecht's own classical introduction—Timon the Misanthrope, an Athenian at the time of the Peloponnesian war—or, as we are better likely to know him from Shakespeare, Timon of Athens.) Horace concludes his Ode thus:

. . . si neque tibias
Euterpe cohibet nec Polyhymnia
Lesboum refugit tendere barbiton.
Quodsi me lyricis vatibus inseres,
sublimi feriam sidera vertice.

Horace longs for the wreath of ivy, the poet's prize, so long as Euterpe does not hold back her flutes nor Polyhymnia refuse to tune the Lesbian lyre for him. But if Maecenas will only place him among the lyric poets, that will be his crowning glory.

It is perhaps telling that in the Hecht, Euterpe makes an appearance, but Polyhymnia does not:

As for me, the prize for poets, the simple gift
For amphybrachs[3] strewn by a kind Euterpe,
With perhaps a laurel crown of the evergreen
Imperishable of your fine endowment
Would supply my modest wants, who dream of nothing
But a pad on Eighth Street and your approbation.

Euterpe is usually the muse of Lyric poetry and Music (though the attributes didn't stabilize until latter antiquity), but one senses that Hecht has in mind the etymology of her name as well—she is the "well-pleasing," the Muse here perhaps of flattery. The omitted (perhaps snubbed) Muse here is, in contrast, Polyhymnia, Muse of Many Hymns, the Muse of the Sublime. Is this an accident? The cynical applicant does not dream of monuments more lasting than bronze, but of a grant that "would supply my modest wants, who dream of nothing/ But a pad on Eighth Street and your approbation." In a devastating (and funny) take on the modern professional poet, the immortal green of the poet's ivy has been

3 I retain the misspelling "amphybrach" for "amphibrach" since it appears thus in *The Venetian Vespers,* and is unchanged in the *Collected* that includes the poem. It seems more likely to be a stubborn typo, however, than a deliberate orthographic quirk.

transformed to greenbacks.

"An Old Malediction" later in the book takes on the Pyrrha Ode (1.5) with the same verve, though to different purpose. As Page points out, 1.5 is "A slight Ode, but singularly beautiful in expression: it is in Horace's best manner as regards style; it is apparently perfectly simple because it is perfectly finished." It's a favorite with translators (John Milton and Christopher Smart, among others).

A sixteen-line Asclepiadean poem in four quatrains, Hecht molds this into the shape and heft of a sonnet—fourteen lines of muscular blank verse. It's a bold but logical formal departure. Many of these shorter love lyrics in Latin function to the modern reader, however anachronistically, as proto-sonnets: of similar length, sonnet-like argument, often containing something of a turn, and already addressed to the cool, fickle, or unattainable mistress—Lesbia, Cynthia, Pyrrha, Lydia—of which Beatrice, Laura, Stella, and assorted other Fair or Dark Mistresses are arguably the avatars. The host of Petrarchan tropes is already in place, down to the rough and fickle seas of love. Here is John Conington's straightforward, rhymed translation in the poetic idiom of 1863:

> What slender youth, besprinkled with perfume,
> Courts you on roses in some grotto's shade?
> Fair Pyrrha, say, for whom
> Your yellow hair you braid,
> So trim, so simple! Ah! how oft shall he
> Lament that faith can fail, that gods can change,
> Viewing the rough black sea
> With eyes to tempests strange,
> Who now is basking in your golden smile,
> And dreams of you still fancy-free, still kind,
> Poor fool, nor knows the guile
> Of the deceitful wind!
> Woe to the eyes you dazzle without cloud
> Untried! For me, they show in yonder fane
> My dripping garments, vow'd
> To Him who curbs the main.

The purpose of a translation is arguably to let us enter a work from which we might otherwise be barred. But the purposes of versions lie elsewhere. Besides being poems "in their own right," they also work as commentaries on the original, while the original may be read as something of a key to their own interpretation.

Part of the pleasure, then, in reading Hecht's version is in how he updates or particularizes or changes the Horatian details. If Horace disapproves of (and envies, and pities) the foppish and callow youngster; Hecht drips with disdain:

What well-heeled knuckle-head, straight from the unisex
Hairstylist and bathed in *Russian Leather,*
Dallies with you these late summer days, Pyrrha,
In your expensive sublet? For whom do you
Slip into something simple, by, say, Gucci?
The more fool he who has mapped out for himself
The saline latitudes of incontinent grief.
Dazzled though he be, poor dope, by the golden looks
Your locks fetched up out of a bottle of *Clairol,*
He will know that the wind changes, the smooth sailing
Is done for, when the breakers wallop him broadside,
When he's rudderless, dismasted, thoroughly swamped
In that mindless riptide that got the best of me
Once, when I ventured on your deeps, Piranha.

Roses become a unisex hair salon, the perfume, "Russian Leather," the pleasant grot, an "expensive sublet." The introduction of "late summer days"—not in Horace—suggests that Pyrrha herself is towards the end of her youth (indeed, her blonde locks are "fetched up out of a bottle of *Clairol").* Part of the Ode's "perfect simplicity" is, indeed, the irony, difficult to capture, in "simplex munditiis"—"simple in its elegance." Here are some other efforts:

"your coil/ of elegant coiffure" (Heather McHugh—"coiffure" is a nice Gallic touch)
"Whose plainness is the pink of taste" (Christopher Smart)
"Plain in thy neatness" (Milton, of whose phrase Page observes that it "savors rather of the Puritan than the poet")

Hecht gets across the irony and then some with: "slip into something simple by, say, Gucci."

Pyrrha is Greek for "flame colored" or "tawny," here perhaps of strawberry-blond hair. It is a common device of Latin love lyric and elegy to give the mistress a Greek nickname—sometimes, as with Catullus's Lesbia, to protect the not-so-innocent—othertimes merely as a convention, with no flesh-and-blood woman in mind, as has sometimes been suggested of Horace. Hecht's retaining of the convention has a triple effect: as a way to pin the poem to the Horace; as a suggestion to the reader that Pyrrha stands in for another name, in this case a modern one; and so that Hecht can metamorphose the femme fatale into a "piranha," a pun that ties wickedly into the nautical language of the end of the poem.

This transformation of a Horatian Ode into a muscular sonnet is something Hecht will demonstrate again in a later book, *Flight Among the Tombs,* which contains a version of Horace's 1.25, "Parcius quatiunt fenestras." If you are only going to choose a handful of Odes to translate in a lifetime, it is a curious selection. As Page puts it: "A coarsely expressed Ode addressed to Lydia, who Horace says will soon be an old woman without the charms, but retaining the passions of her youth, and destined to meet with the same haughty contempt she now employs towards her lovers. It has no merit and may be omitted with advantage." (Indeed, John Conington *does* omit it.) Here is an accomplished verse-rendering by Len Krisak, faithful except insofar as it grants the translation more charm than the original:

> The brash young men come less and less to toss
> Their pebbles at your shutters, than before.
> They let you sleep now, so there's little loss.
>   The doorjamb hugs that door
>
> That used to swing so freely on its hinges.
> Now lovers never cry your name and weep,
> "O Lydia, all night long your hard heart swinges
>   Mine! Oh, how can you sleep?"
>
> Some day your turn will come. You'll be a crone,
> Sobbing in alleys, "Men!" It's coming soon—
> That night when Thracian winds grow mad and moan
>   Beneath a missing moon,
>
> And love is lust and lust is wild desire
> That blows through mares in heat just like a gale,
> And sets your lacerated heart on fire.
>   Then, Lydia, you'll wail
>
> That young men like their ivy green, preferring
> What's fresh; that lustrous myrtle's what they love.
> Dry husks are Eurus's—that cold, bleak whirring
>   They'll be the playthings of.

Hecht's approach is something of the opposite—he pushes the poem into greater "coarseness":

> The Whirligig of Time
>
> They are fewer these days, those supple, suntanned boys
> Whose pebbles tapped at your window, and your door
> Swings less and less on its obliging hinges
> For wildly importunate suitors. Fewer the cries

Of "Lydia, how can you sleep when I've got the hots?
I won't last out the night; let me get my rocks off."
Things have moved right along, and, behold, it's you
Who quails, like a shriveled whore, as they scorn and dodge you,
And the wind shrieks like a sex-starved thing in heat
As the moon goes dark and the mouth of your old dry vulva
Rages and hungers, and your worst, most ulcerous pain
Is knowing those sleek-limbed boys prefer the myrtle,
The darling buds of May, leaving dried leaves
To cluster in unswept corners, fouling doorways.

Hecht serves us notice that this is not merely an exercise in translation with the title—a quotation from Shakespeare's Twelfth Night ("the whirligig of time brings in his revenges")—the menacing motto of the poem.

In the opening, Hecht hews closely to the original: no brand names here. At the beginning, it is only the addition of "suntanned" that suggests this is as much about the present day as Augustan Rome. The coolly Latinate "obliging" is brilliant for "facilis" (the easy hinges), getting across the personification of the door with all of its sexual connotation. The personification, including sometimes the direct address, of the lover's door is actually part of the tradition of a genre of poems and songs, the *paraklausithyron*—a song sung outside a lover's closed door, usually after the suitor has been out to a drinking party. The mood of such songs is one of drunken sentimentality and self-pity, grafted onto inebriated horniness, and brings with it the bathetic image of the lover with a wreath of bedraggled flowers on his head slumping asleep in the doorway. Horace may actually be quoting such a song when he has the lover declare: "Me tuo longas pereunte noctes, Lydia, dormis?" (Do you sleep, Lydia, while I, your lover, am pining away through the endless nights?)

In short, it's the rhetoric and language of pop music, which is why Hecht's sudden shift into the jaunty slang of sexual conquest ("Lydia, how can you sleep when I've got the hots?/ I won't last out the night. Let me get my rocks off") seems both shocking *and* surprisingly appropriate. In Horace, the simple future tense (flebis, "you will weep" in your turn someday) sets up the eventual "revenges" of time. Hecht does something different. He fast-forwards, so Lydia can see the future for herself. The future has already arrived, in the perfect and then the present tense: "Things have moved right along, and behold, it's you. . . ."

The sexual appetite of mares in heat was proverbial in ancient times—hippomanes, an ointment derived from mares in oestrous, was a legendary aphrodisiac/love-potion, and this reference to Lydia's brute sexuality is in no way complimentary. Hecht seems to take it even further, however, to a "sex-starved *thing* in heat." Horace has "sub inter-/ lunia," the dark nights before the new moon appears; Hecht has "as the moon goes dark" but adds "and the mouth of your old dry vulva/ Rages and hungers," an image almost violent in its disgust. This is not, obviously, in the original, though perhaps suggested by the wind raving like a bacchante (an image of female irrationality and appetite). And indeed, the Hecht makes me look at the Horace a little differently—wondering whether the dark of the moon, besides being atmospheric and, as commentators point out, associated with shifts in weather—does not also carry with it an adumbration of menopause, something to consider, perhaps, even in the extreme enjambment (though a convention in Sapphics) that interrupts the word "interlunia."

Hecht's "ulcerous," for all its ugliness, comes more or less directly from Horace: "saeviet circa iecur ulcerosum"—which may be translated as, lust "will rage around your wounded heart"; but more technically, around your "ulcerous" "impassioned" or "inflamed" liver. It was in the liver that the ancients located the seat of anger and other passions (hence "bilious"); this amounts to our metaphorical use of "heart," but retains also about it something of the anatomy lecture, which Hecht matches and even exceeds in the clinically correct "vulva." Further, in English, "ulcerous" might bring to mind physical ulcers—perhaps even sexually transmitted disease. Yet, just when the poem seems to have crossed the line from coarseness to outright misogyny, Hecht reminds us of the layers of remove again with another reference to Shakespeare, "the darling buds of May," from the famous sonnet, XVIII, "Shall I compare thee to a summer's day?" with its warning that "summer's lease hath all too short a date" and "every fair from fair sometime declines." Shakespeare's solution to this is to immortalize his love in verse. It's an ironic poem to bring into the mix. Lydia too will be immortalized, but not for her beauty.

There are three other translations from Horace in Hecht's corpus, appearing side by side in *The Darkness and the Light:* "A Symposium," Horace 1.27, "A Special Occasion," 3.21, and "A Prayer for Twin Divinities," 1.21. These are all straightforward, if extremely lively and accomplished—the first two in limber blank verse, the last in envelope-rhymed quatrains. Being translations rather than versions, they offer less scope in a sense for peering into the poet's process, aside perhaps for admiring the vigor and beauty of certain turns of phrase, such as the astonishing "Till Phoebus, with punctual bustle, banishes starlight." One is a conversational drinking song urging Epicurean moderation, one a birthday poem that might (I imagine) have appealed to Hecht on the occasion of an actual birthday. "A Prayer to Twin Divinities" is a curiously minor ode to translate, especially since Hecht does it so straightforwardly, charming though his rhymed version is. Page mentions that Orelli is "probably right in considering the Ode too slight to have been written for any great public occasion," though Franke suggested it was at the institution of games in memory of the battle of Actium. It is a pledge to civilization and a charm against war. If anything, though, Hecht tones even this last down, omitting the epithet "lacrimosum" before "bellum"—a translation in itself of Homer, "war full of tears."

I would argue that Hecht's idiosyncratic selection of some of the less famous Odes speaks of an early and intimate acquaintance with the Odes (mostly, I presume, with Book One) in the original. Though Hecht does not speak of a classical education, he remarks to Philip Hoy of his otherwise lackluster school days that, "the Latin and math teachers were severe but kind." Perhaps he was attracted to Horace as a schoolboy for reasons of temperament as well as for their singular graces and beauties. But as an adult, he might have been struck more strongly with their similarities. Both are poets of great virtuosity and wide-ranging learning, who had seen war and its devastations firsthand, and were all the more attracted to civilization with a small and a capital C, to the humane republic of letters, which survives the rise and fall of empires.

★★★

Sources Cited

Bennett, Charles E., trans., *Horace Odes & Epodes.* New York: Caratzas Brothers Publishers, 1988.

Connington, John, trans., *The Odes and Carmen Saeculare of Horace.* London: Bell & Daldy, 1872.

Hecht, Anthony, *Collected Earlier Poems,* New York: Alfred A. Knopf, 1990.

Hecht, Anthony, *Collected Later Poems.* New York: Alfred A. Knopf, 2003.

Hoy, Philip, *Anthony Hecht in conversation with Philip Hoy.* London: Between the Lines, 1999.

Krisak, Len, ed. and trans., *The Odes of Horace, in Latin and English.* Manchester: Carcanet 2006.

Lewis, Peter, and Caroline Lewis, eds., *Sappho Through English Poetry.* London: Anvil Press, 1996.

McClatchy, J.D., ed. *Horace, The Odes: New Translations by Contemporary Poets.* Princeton, NJ: Princeton University Press, 2002.

Page, T.E., ed., *Q. Horatii Flacci Carminum Libri IV Epodon Liber.* London: Macmillian 1964.

Poole, Adrian, and Jeremy Maule, eds., *The Oxford Book of Classical Verse in Translation.* Oxford: Oxford University Press, 1995.

Blaine Vitallo

The Color Blue

See us walking through the sunshine
Ask me "Where I've been?"
Back to the Ire?
Back to desire
This is where it all begins!
— The Joy Formidable, "This Ladder Is Ours"

She was fond of walking on the rooftop, dangerously close to the edge. She'd laugh if you asked why.

Her hair was sapphire. He loved the color and thought it wonderful in his hands.

"Do you like them?" she asked, staring wide.

He said of course, but the color unnerved him. Yellow eyes weren't natural.

She'd been muttering in her sleep. He'd reached across the bed and touched her shoulder, hoping it was normal.

But let's face it, she was never normal.

He was sitting beside her, looking at the stars.

"I watched you from them," she said. "That one, to be precise. Yes, I saw you from the heavens and loved you right away." She was breathing deep.

He looked into her yellow eyes but didn't cry.

She was smiling so wonderfully. Who could tell her otherwise?

"I know you did," he said. "I felt it."

She leaned on his shoulder. Her hair smelled of starlight.

The house was too narrow for its height. He hated to watch her when she was up there. But she danced so gracefully. Once, he nearly called for her but held his tongue. What if she turned and fell? If only he could catch her.

She was falling, though. Just not her body.

"You know I came for you?" she said, wrapping her arms around his shoulders. Her chin rested near his neck. Her fingers interlaced over his chest.

She was so warm.

"I saw you and came first thing because love is like that." She laughed.

He put his hands over hers.

Just don't say it, just don't say it.

She kissed his neck. Her blue hair spilled down his arm.

"It most certainly is," he said.

Another day. She was up on the roof again. More and more she was there. He wrung his hands. He should call her down.

He held the box of hair dye. He loved the color, but maybe if he got rid of it.

No, it was those damned contacts. They were so yellow.

No, it was him.

He came up behind her. His arms encircled her waist.

She wriggled to get free, but he held on, laughing. She laughed too, and he loved it. Her joy was sweet.

When she came down, she stood barefoot on the swing. She was little on the inside. He'd read that was often the case.

She looked determined.

He sat picking dandelions in the grass. The shade was nice. The white house looked too hot in the sunshine.

"If I swung a little higher, I could go home!"

"You most certainly could, my darling," he said frowning.

She pouted, sitting in the therapist's chair. He ground his teeth, thinking she hated him for this.

"And you're from where?" the therapist asked, adjusting her glasses.

She crossed her arms and frowned.

"Please tell her," he said, hating himself.

"We're more advanced than you are," she blurted out.

He sighed, but when they got home it didn't matter. She cried, and her eyes were filled with fear.

He pressed himself to her, and eventually she was happy again.

But he hated to let go. If no one held her she might fall off the roof.

She slurped melted ice cream from her bowl. "I guess I love it because we don't have food like this."

"In the heavens?" he said, staring at his spoon, then her.

She smiled so wide he thought he'd die.

"It's a lovely, blue ball," she said, watching a bird.

The damn house felt alive. It had roots. He only liked it for her. She felt free here.

The country has that effect. It's like no one else exists.

To her no one really did, except for him.

The windows watched like eyes. They were always fixed on her as she ambled through the yard and ate picnics on a blanket.

Sometimes he watched her too, from inside, where he wouldn't have to share her joy. It was poison.

Those eyes were so yellow. He saw them sweep him up and down as they stood next to each other in the mirror. She clasped her hands behind her back and examined herself. She kicked her dress across the floor and smiled sly.

Her skin felt so soft.

"It's like that because of our water," she said, pulling his hand up her side. "We're all this soft."

He kissed her and said he knew. She'd told him before.

She was dancing on the roof again, spinning and smiling. Her feet were on the edge. She watched the stars. She always watched the stars.

"But who can look away from home?" she asked.

He thought of their green shutters and grimaced.

He took a step closer but didn't move again. He was shaking.

"Don't worry," she said. "Everyone must visit home."

"Just come with me," he said. "This is home."

The sky would be gray tomorrow. She wouldn't see the stars that day.

"It has to be now!" she shouted, spinning faster. She was so light on her feet.

In another life she had been fond of dancing on stage.

Seclusion, it seemed, was not the cure.

"I can fly, you know?" she said, the starlight gleaming in her eyes.

They used to be blue, like her hair.

It *was* the dye. She'd been fine before that. But he loved the color and had encouraged her.

"I really can," she said, stopping on the ledge. She turned to face him.

"I believe you," he said crying.

"Aw, don't weep, my love." She smiled and clasped her hands behind her. "I'll be back before you know it."

"No!"

She stepped backwards.
The sky proved too gray. He watched nothing but clouds.
Maybe she was there, watching him again.
Yes, she most certainly was, he thought as he set a dandelion by the stone.

Rory Waterman

A Review of Philip Gross, *Deep Field*

Bloodaxe, 2011

ISBN 978-1-85224-919-9 (Hardcover), UK £8.95

★★★

In advanced old age, Philip Gross's father was afflicted with deafness and aphasia, and *Deep Field* is the poet's book-length response. Its poems (the majority of which are the sections of three sequences called "Something Like the Sea" parts I, II and III) comprise one interwoven work of warm remembrance and strikingly cool analysis. Aphasia, he writes, is "like the sea"—but "don't imagine that I mean it/ beautifully." Rather, both are (indeed) estranging, entropic:

> it's in the dissolution business,
> particles suspended for a while
>
> round sunken matter, dis-
> cohering, smoking off in strands,
>
> and don't imagine that I want
> to go there.

At one point in the collection, Gross compares the predicament of this father and son to two people stranded on opposite shores, just beyond the point of communication. At another, he notes that "you've un-aged into chatterbox child," and have become "at home/ in the body now it's leaving you." In "Mule" the poet evokes "your heart," before stating in an aside "I'm not talking poetry here// but infarct and scar tissue." But this book is full of metaphorical heart too.

The sea is one leitmotif in *Deep Field;* the "deep field" of space is another. Both are ever-present but inscrutable frontiers. The title poem finds Hubble

> like you
> adrift
> because no
> direction is *not* down,
> or up, and so
> we stumble.

Gross is fascinated by the liminal: thresholds of language, geography, nature, belonging—even "the edge of meaning," as he puts it in "Something Like the Sea II." This was evident in *The Water Table,* which won the T.S. Eliot Prize in 2009. *Deep Field* revivifies such concerns through the prism of personal loss, of a kind to which many of us can, sadly, relate on some level. "There has to be a country," one section begins,

> in which what you have for speech
> is language.
> Swamp land, surely. Or
> unsurely, because channels shift.

These poems are united by their theme and quest, of course. But they move between perspectives, each seeming to tack in a different direction to the last. Gross circles his theme with a relentlessness and ingenuity that withstands comparison to the way Tennyson circles his in "In Memoriam," replete with bittersweet memories of the irrecoverable past, memories which come freighted with painful doses of irony:

> each wave a slap in the face,
> beside you. Then not. It had me by the ankles,
> the undertow, dragging us out and apart, and all
> I could clutch for was your voice. I caught one word
> *Float!* and it brought me back to shore.

This book concentrates on a horror that is as mundane as it is awful: this demise is not the death of a premature child, the sudden illness of a once-athletic middle-aged partner, a heroic slaughtering. This is a quiet falling apart of the sort we are accustomed to thinking about as little as possible, but which is all around us. For this reason more than any other *Deep Field* has the feel of a book destined quietly to be forgotten about. But it is also a finely balanced accomplishment, as inventive and even celebratory as it is chilling, and those who miss it miss out.

Donna Laemmlen

Crown of Iguanas

Socorro hadn't intended to steal the iguana. She only wanted a few of her things back, the camera her cousin had sent her from Sonora, the cast-iron tortilla pan from her sister, the vibrant orange and yellow weavings from her trip to Chiapas. After three months of marriage, she realized her husband was torpid and callous and preferred cocooning in his hammock with his prized reptile than in bed with her. She had been right to abandon him, but she hadn't meant to shame him in that way.

When they had lived together, Socorro had cared for his iguana, feeding it lettuce and radishes, stroking its scaly head and mopping its puddles of urine from the linoleum. She had let it crawl up her arm and onto her head more times than she could remember. On clarion days, she paraded it on a string along the country road in front of their cottage or in the marketplace on the edge of town. They had once ventured into the zócalo for the Radish Festival (she thought he might enjoy the elaborate carvings), but he had swiped the crown from the "Our Lady of Solitude" sculpture and ripped it to shreds in seconds. That had caused an embarrassing uproar.

If the iguana hadn't leaped from the curtains and onto her head when she snuck in to reclaim her belongings, Socorro might not have acted out of spite, wrapping her shawl around her head, around the iguana, hiding it there, ruining her life. How many were there now? Five? Six? She didn't dare look in a mirror, and no one was brave enough to count them for her; they were all afraid of turning into iguanas themselves.

Now, with each step Socorro took into town, the iguanas dug their toenails in deeper. Their constant swaying and jockeying for room in her black curly hair made her so nauseous she hoped candied ginger from the market would settle her stomach. They had become so fat and comfortable, plucking cantaloupe and watermelon from street vendors, snagging lettuce from tacos and salads, she had difficulty holding her head up, and her scalp itched like crazy.

Socorro had tried to train the iguanas to help her with her chores. After all, she reasoned, if they were going to impose themselves on her, they should at least learn a useful skill. But that had been disastrous. They couldn't launder the clothes because their claws ripped them to shreds; they couldn't garden because they ate all the vegetables; they couldn't cook for the same reason. Socorro had become a strict carnivore because of them. They couldn't sweep or dust or shop. Within a month, they had become a pile of apathetic lazybones, just like her husband.

It was late afternoon by the time Socorro reached the marketplace. She scurried through the aisles as best she could, searching near the tamarind, the chocolate, the turmeric, but without one brave vendor to help her, her right hip and knee suddenly buckled from the slippery weight and she dropped onto a bucket of flour to rest.

The iguanas didn't mind waiting. They enjoyed looking at the colorful piñatas that twirled in the air, listening to the parakeets that sang from their cages. They bounced to the rhythm of mariachis playing their trumpets. They turned a basket of toasted grasshoppers into shambles as it passed by. Two of them worked together to steal a whole mango, and they all relished the mess they made eating it.

When Socorro rested so long she couldn't carry them anymore, the iguanas were finally forced to do something. After intense deliberation, they scavenged a hemp rope from a cobblestone gutter and tied it around Socorro's neck. They weren't worried about her creeping through the market or moseying along the jutted country road. They knew it would be dark long before they returned to their increasingly cramped cottage. But they were worried about feeding her; they didn't know the first thing about meat.[4]

4 "In 'Crown of Iguanas,' the image of the iguanas unfolds with the logic of a good dream, creating a ending that is both surprising and relevant."—Thaisa Frank, Final Judge, 2013 Able Muse Write Prize (for Fiction) on this winning story, "Crown of Iguanas," by Donna Laemmlen.

Marly Youmans

Waterborne

— From "The Baby and the Bathwater"

Let it go, let it all go down the drain—
Ash from the crossroads where a witch was burned,
Dirt from the cellar where a queen was slain,
No heir escaping death, and nothing learned,

The crescent moons of darkness under nails,
Ditch-digger's drops of sweat, the blood from soil
That sprouted fingertips, the slick from snails
Glinting on butchered peasants left to spoil:

Let it swirl, let it all swirl down the drain—
Let murderous grime be curlicues to gyre
Around the blackened mouth, let mortal bane
Be gulped, and waste be drink for bole and briar.

Here's a new-washed babe; marvel what man mars,
The flesh so innocent it gleams like stars.

Anna M. Evans

Prague Spring

A barrow boy is juggling with pears
before a girl whose scarf and white capris
seem more like something Audrey Hepburn wears.
A group of urchins huddle on their knees
around a baseball card that someone earned
showing U.S. tourists round the city.
An old man grins as though he has just learned
he isn't dying. On the lake a pretty
becalmed sailboat tacks its stately dance.
A busking violinist pauses, dreaming
of playing Beethoven in Paris, France.
The façade of *Hotel Evropa*'s gleaming
in August sunshine like a golden pin.
And then the tanks roll in.

John Savoie

Winter of Discontent

He shuffles, slides,
drags his IV—

this one leans,
that one totters—

all the way
to the window

to watch the glistening
icicles drip.

Charles Wilkinson

Is There Anybody There?

Thronging the faint moonbeams on the dark stair
— Walter de la Mare, "The Listeners"

Once she could no longer manage the stairs, the ghosts moved down from the attic and the little box room at the top of the house. They had been living among long-discarded Christmas decorations, leather albums—photographs of the sepia dead—battered suitcases that had been filled with clothes for holidays that had been taken fifty years ago or more. Some, perhaps the shyest, rested in the white dust that stretched over the wooden floorboards; a few lurked in the cobwebs braided over low beams and rafters, and there was one that pressed its nose against a tiny skylight, or tapped thin fingers on the glass, as if hungry to be dispersed amongst the stars.

Mrs. G had arranged for her bed and a chest of drawers to be moved into what was once a living room at the front of the house. The scullery had been converted into a shower with rails to prevent her from falling. From the kitchen, she had a view of the back garden: high grass; the web of the dead hedge killed by a winter frost; patches of cold evergreen, the half-healed birch trees tissued with silver scars; a birdbath that she knew was filled with thin brown water, a few twigs and a leaf shaped like a goldfish: everything neglected since the death of the Irish gardener who had looked after it all for a quarter of a century or more.

Although her eyesight was dim unless she remembered to put on her spectacles, and even then the edges were slightly blurred, less sharp than they had been just a year ago, she could still hear the sound of the letter box being pushed open and the slither and clunk of the mail dropping to the floor. She shuffled into the hall. There were the usual catalogs sent by clothes companies and one letter. She recognized the hand with its strange loops and shiny black ink immediately; and, since she knew that what was written there was her own name and address, it seemed as if she were able to read it without her glasses. The stamp proved that the sender was no longer in America; indeed, the postmark suggested that he was now, most unfortunately, here—in Birmingham. A flutter of perturbation. At first, her bent fingers seemed incapable of opening the envelope, but then a thumbnail worked its way under the flap and a moment later, she found her spectacles, which for once had been attached to the cord that she wore round her neck. There were three sheets of paper closely covered in the familiar tangle of letters, with the gs and ys stroked like nooses. At first, she had been pleased that someone was taking an interest in Keidrych's work after all these years. She had responded helpfully to this American professor who was employed at a university she had never heard of. Then the project on which her correspondent was at work changed from being a critical edition of the work—apparently someone else had already almost completed this—to a full-scale biography. The questions, the requests for documents and introductions to friends of the poet, most of whom had turned out to have been dead for many years, became more insistent and intrusive; once there had even been a phone call and a request for information of a deeply personal nature. And now this man had established himself in a hotel that was not at all far away and was proposing that he should visit her. She had no sooner decided that she would not even bother to reply when she realized that silence could either be mistaken for assent or create a mystery that the professor would feel compelled to solve. Then she would end up answering phone calls or find the man and his tape recorder camped on her doorstep. She went to her table in the living room and began to write.

Dear Professor Hopton,

I hope that you will not take umbrage when I say that not only I am unable to receive you here, but it will also be impossible for me to take up your kind invitation to visit you at the hotel where you are staying. I am in my ninety-first year and at present without help in the house or garden. My state of health is such that even those activities that I am still fortunate enough to engage in are strictly circumscribed. I was glad to learn that your motivation for visiting us here in the city of Birmingham is not solely a desire to learn more about my relationship with the poet Keidrych Gomer-Price. In truth, it was of short duration and of no great intensity on either side: almost, one might say, something less than a dalliance. I have sent you, I believe, copies of all of the poems, whether in manuscript form or published in the fugitive literary journals of those days, which are in my possession. I must reiterate that, contrary to your suspicions, I have none of Keidrych's letters. Assuming my recollections are correct, we seldom corresponded—if at all. When one remembers that during the time of our greatest intimacy, we were both resident in the same quarter of Birmingham and seeing each other almost daily, this is surely not surprising. It is possible that we exchanged a few cards when I went up to Cambridge, but I never received either the passionate outpourings or the detailed exposition of his poetics that you imagine.

Since you persist in believing that I have been less than candid with you, I will set down here those of my impressions of Keidrych that might reasonably be thought of interest. I have not kept copies of my previous letters to you, and if some of what I write here either overlaps with, or even contradicts, the material that I sent you, you must put this down to the fallible memory of a very old woman.

It was winter when we met, introduced by a friend as we came out of one of the organ concerts given in the Town Hall. It was a cold day and I remember not only Keidrych's kind, sensitive face and his hair worn just slightly too long, like that of the pilots who were soon to defend our shores, but also the bright stripes of his scarf: color against a backdrop of blackened terra-cotta and the gray stone of the quasi-Athenian Town Hall. And the way that he moved with a nonchalant ease, an animal quite comfortable in its habitat. In spite of his name and background, his accent was not markedly Welsh, though there was a musicality in his phrasing that was somehow un-English.

We walked round to the reference library and as we ascended the marble staircase, exchanged whispered comments about the concert and the names of poets that we were reading; it soon became evident what a wealth of enthusiasms we shared. We agreed to meet the next day. I remember a café, long since disappeared, in one of the roads that led down to New Street, but I cannot recall what was said. It was not long after this occasion that Keidrych showed me some of his poems. Although I already had an acquaintance with Mr. Eliot's work, my teachers having been more alert to modernist developments in the arts than most, I was quite unprepared for the astounding verbal density, the proliferating plurality of meanings, the quotations in languages with which I was unfamiliar and the wildly unorthodox typography that characterized my friend's writing. I recollect sitting in his small room in a suburb of south Birmingham, turning the pages of the manuscript back and forth, desperately searching for a single line on which I could make a comment that was sensible let alone true. The silence lengthened. Outside the window, a blackbird sang a cappella. I sensed, I believe, something of the lyrical force of Keidryich's work, but his words were no more than notes on a score given to one who does not read music. As he sat on the edge of a small table by the window and looked down on me shuffling through the pages, and glancing up at him from time to time, no doubt with stark bewilderment in my eyes, the afternoon sunlight threaded the crown of his head with hairs of gold. Then he stepped down easily, both feet falling to the floor as if they were padded like a gentle animal's, and softly took his work from my hands; with the slightest sad smile on his lips, he put it into the bottom drawer of the desk from which he had taken it. After that day, although he gave me a signed copy of his first volume, he never again made any attempt to discuss his work with me. It was only after his death that some of his manuscripts came into my possession.

★★★

Towards evening Mrs. G became aware of the ghosts gathering at the top of the stairs. She thought that she heard one of them creak slowly down three or four steps, like a timid child who is uncertain whether or not to join a party below. Then it lost its nerve and scurried quickly back up to rejoin the dead. Some nights she thought that she could hear music being played very quietly, half-familiar songs that might have been popular in her childhood. A neighbor had told her that a light was being switched on and off in a room at the very top of the house, but when she persuaded a friend to come round and check, nothing was amiss. There wasn't even a bulb in the socket. After that it had seemed best to ignore their all too predictable activities.

As she picked up the beginning of her letter to Professor Hopton, she heard the tread of footsteps in the empty room above and a cough that sounded like the one her father had developed in the months before he died. Outside, daylight refused to dwindle, and she could see the youths scuffling and promenading in the streets. She was glad that it was still just a little too cold for them to sit on the wall, drinking cans of beer or sharing a huge plastic bottle of cider. Everything that she had written to Professor Hopton was true and none of it was of any importance. She looked at her glass-fronted bookcase: her Larousse was still there, not used for years but still smudged by her kitchen-sticky fingers; the novels by Hardy and Dickens; the first editions of Eliot, Rose Macaulay and de la Mare; then beneath them the lives of great men bound in leather, their long chapters locked in, inert and unstained on the shelf.

It was the week before she had been due to go up to Cambridge that, finding herself in the street where Keidrych had his lodgings, she decided to visit him unexpectedly. After the landlady let her in, she made her way up to the top of the house, where Keidrych had his room. She knocked and waited for him to answer the door, imagining his pale melancholy features breaking into a smile at her unexpected arrival. Almost a minute went by before she heard the sound of movement and hushed voices from within. Then the door opened to reveal a young man in a dressing gown, his blond hair tufted and askew as if he had only just risen from his bed. His face was very smooth, almost mask-like, making his lips seem fuller and his eyes appear like gems that had been inserted into his head. She could no longer remember what words they had exchanged. No doubt she had been told that Keidrych was not at home. She could, however, recall that it was only afterwards—when she was back down in the street, with the trees, the light, the houses somehow stranger than before, as if they had been borrowed from a film made in the area but which she had not yet seen—that she realized that the young man had been wearing make-up.

She put down her unfinished letter, went over to the bureau and unlocked the small drawer at the top. She took out a ring and put it on. It was far too large for her shrunken finger. If she had tried to wear it for long, it would soon have fallen off. It had, she supposed, been her good fortune that she had visited him that day. Discovered his true nature before anyone, apart from her parents, had been told of the engagement. Keidrych and she had discussed the matter as dispassionately as their temperaments allowed. It had been kind of him to insist that she keep the ring. She read three of his letters, although she already knew the words by heart and then put everything back in the drawer. A finger on her right hand was inflamed with arthritis and she felt a sharp pain as she turned the key.

The laughter and cries of the youths died away down the street, but now there was a someone standing by the iron gate in her front garden. She put on her glasses, and the smudged shape redefined itself as a man with pepper and salt hair and lean features. He appeared well dressed in a camel-hair coat and was looking around, searching, no doubt, for the number of the house. Her diary was on the top of the bureau and open. She turned a page and saw "Professor Hopton. 6 o'clock p.m."

It was an appointment that she had no recollection of making, but the hand was undoubtedly hers, each thorny letter in black ink imbued with the pain it cost her to write it. As she made her way back towards the hall, she heard the clang of the gate and the sound of quick footsteps on the path. By the time she made her way to the living room door, she could see his corrugated, twisting figure through the waves of frosted glass. The bell rang. If she went on into the hall, he would hear her and maybe even catch a glimpse of her trying to reach the sanctuary of the kitchen. She stood quite still. She knew that the ghosts had come down, some of them from the very top of the house, and were sitting huddled together on the staircase, although a few of the less bold were leaning against the banisters on the first floor landing, waiting for her to open the door. The bell rang again and then after a moment there were three sharp raps. She was reminded of a poem that she had read in her childhood. Soon she would no longer be a part of the world of men. Something seemed to disturb the ghosts and the air shivered around her as she listened with them.

There were three more knocks, a silence and then his voice: "Is there anybody there?" More silence. "Well, can you tell Mrs. G that I came."

The footsteps retreated down the path, the gate clanged. When Mrs. G stepped into the hall, there were no dark shapes behind the frozen ripples of glass. Silence thickened about her, as if she were underwater.

★★★

That night it was cold in the corner of the living room. Her sheets felt clammy and the ache in her hand and knees was worse. The plaster on the ground floor had soaked up the damp from the cellar, and now the wallpaper was stenciled and water stained with the shores of continents that had come up from below, superimposing themselves on the patterns of faded-to-pastel flowers. Slowly she levered herself off the bed. During the day she covered it with a bright rug so that it looked like a divan. Once she had steadied herself and found her stick, she negotiated a way through the furniture, some of which she had arranged to be brought down from her bedroom, and into the kitchen. The kettle's breath was soon visible, but the pain in her fingers dimmed as the hot-water bottle filled. As she made her way back to the living room, she reminded herself that it was in that room that her parents had met Keidrych Gomer-Price for the only time. An afternoon of bone china, napkins folded into neat pyramids, triangular sandwiches with paste and wafer-thin bread. A huge silver teapot and sugar cubes in a Royal Worcester bowl. Heavy hallmarked cutlery. Slow conversation with long pauses in which to hear the traffic and a bird singing. Keidrych's hair an inch too long and his tie a shade too bright. His hairy tweed jacket dug out from the back of the wardrobe, the shoes polished but worn, the wilted corn of the corduroy trousers: the bohemian aping respectability. And afterwards, when he had gone, the washing up and the hints that she would find someone better. But she never had. Not anyone.

The hot water bottle warmed her as she burrowed herself into the hollow of the mattress. She held the rubber against her knees while the heat worked its way into her until it almost burnt. Then she drew it up to her breasts and let it lie against her like a lover, while it slowly cooled to the temperature of flesh. She was safe now, deeply entrenched in a tunnel of blankets and sheets.

He joined her in the early hours, not disturbing the earth as he slipped in beside her. His body was cool and she could feel the ribs of his chest. This was what she had always longed for: to hold him, quite naked, in her arms. The love grew, swelled to desire, until it became almost pain; then was pain itself, pain merging with love, carrying her for the moment beyond thought and memory, sweeping her into the furthest and darkest corners of the night.

★★★

The next morning she awoke early. A crack in the curtains let in a knife of sunlight to slice the room in two. There was a bright day outside, waiting to enter. Her pain had quite gone and when she rose she could not hear the customary creak of her joints or the scrape of bone against bone. Her movements seemed effortless, almost liquid in their fluency. When she was halfway to the table, she realized that she had not even looked round for her stick. The memory of the previous night had left a slow lingering joy, the sense that something greatly longed for had now at last been fulfilled. With gratitude, she glanced back towards her bed. There was a hump beneath the blankets, which at first she mistook for a pillow. But as she focused her attention on the shape, she saw that it was the outline of a body curled between the sheets like a cat. She remembered how supple he had been, the grace of his walk. It hardly seemed possible that he should still be here. But there was no sign of a head. Perhaps it was just the imprint of her own body, preserving the space where she had slept.

The unfinished letter was spread out on the table where she had left it. She read through it again. Almost every sentence was measured, dead with a dull formality—or strangely irrelevant. Why had she mentioned the blackbird? The only life was in the very smallest details. The scarf that he had left accidentally at her house on the day he had met her parents for the only time. It was made of a very soft material, cashmere not silk. It had probably been the most expensive garment he had owned. He'd been so relieved when she returned it the next day. "Documents in my possession." How cold. What she had always wanted was to possess and be possessed. Now was the time to tear it up and begin again. There was so much that she knew about him that would be lost forever if she did not write it down. Her pen was lying right next to the last sheet of paper, but her fingers were not moving towards it. Now that she thought of it she realized that she could not feel either of her arms at all. She made a conscious effort to stretch out her right hand and pick up the pen. Nothing happened. Perhaps the night had been much colder than she had realized. The thing to do would be to go into the kitchen and warm herself by the stove. Her legs still seemed to be carrying her, the air parting to let her through without the slightest resistance. That was a relief. As she entered the kitchen, she had a clear view of the garden. Summer seemed to have come early to it, flowers had appeared from nowhere overnight, and she could see the Irishman contentedly edging the lawn. But it was only when she saw her mother, bending over the range as she stirred invisible soup, that Mrs. G understood.

★★★

After she rose on the warmth of her death, the last heat of energy's dispersal, she found herself next to the spider in the attic. A companion of sorts. Trapped in its own web, its long legs were delicate, silvered with dust, its abdomen still as a brooch. At first she did not see the boy floating by the skylight, the thin fingers that tapped on the glass; even the outline of his torso was no more than a floater disturbing the edge of vision, less than a watermark on white paper that is raised to the sun. But then she knew that he had been waiting here. Out of time, would she remember his short story? Had he lived in these rooms, played on the lawn, looked over the hedge in the front garden, walked in gray Midland daylight? Or was he perhaps only an idea? The child she might have had with Kheidrych? His faint noise an echo of an impulse that had died before birth.

In the living room her pen lies at an angle next to the letter. Soon they will find the flesh that housed her world curled under the sheets. No longer trapped by tense, does she know the present? The professor's plane waits on the runway; in his suitcase, under his pyjamas, sits his manuscript and its many words in search of a phantom subject. The plane will begin to taxi along the runway, but there will be that ambiguous instant when he is not sure whether he has taken off or is still in touch with the ground.

Ghosts are gathering at the head of the dark staircase, though this one, whom nobody remembers, is free to go; the last thought on earth that anyone had of it has escaped into the throng of moonbeams, not staying for an archived name. Now the least timid spirits have at last made their way into the living room. There is one that stretches out a hand to touch the furniture she once knew; another waits in the hall for a knock from the world of men. But these shades are hovering by the bookshelf, alone in invisible yearning, as if they could wait for centuries for a page to bring them to life.

Jane Hammons

A Review of Nina Schuyler, *The Translator*

Pegasus Books, 2013

ISBN 978-1-60598-470-4 (Hardcover), USA $25.00

★★★

At fifty-four Hanne Schubert, the protagonist of Nina Schuyler's intelligent, complex new novel, *The Translator,* hopes to achieve wide acclaim with the translation of a novel by Japanese writer, Yukio Kobayashi. The translation is so critical to Hanne's sense of accomplishment and worth that Schuyler opens her novel with a passage from it. Jiro, the main character, describes his wife Aiko, who has just crashed her car into the garage door:

> Her white-knuckled hands grip the wheel. . . . Her self-inflicted paralysis leaches into him and turns him into stone. Last night in bed she told him again that her heart was punctured and her life was slowly dripping out of her. 'What do you want me to do?' he said, not bothering to hide his frustration.

"'*Iradachi,*' the Japanese word for frustration." Schuyler deftly weaves Hanne's translation into the text, allowing us to understand Hanne, in part, through the work that is so important to her. We see her consider meaning, test words and phrases against her understanding of Jiro, whom she takes possession of in the process of translation, creating a rich fantasy life in which she imagines she is having sex with him when she is with her lover, David.

"Of course you are frustrated, Jiro," Hanne says aloud, sympathizing with him as though he is in her presence. Jiro's frustration with his wife Aiko is similar to the frustration that Hanne feels toward her adult daughter, Brigitte. The two have been estranged for six years, ever since Hanne sent an adolescent Brigitte away from their home in San Francisco to a strict boarding school in Connecticut.

> [Aiko] doesn't appear to be physically harmed; and that's the problem, he thinks. The harm is tucked deep inside. She's seen dozens of doctors who've given so many different diagnoses, yet her hurt remains nameless.

Naming things is not only Hanne's job, but her belief in the power of language to give meaning and expression to all experience, often without consideration of the way emotions inform perception and understanding, making her seem at first rigid, even cold. But in addition to Brigitte, Hanne has a son, Tomas, who is several years older than his sister. Hanne is close to him and his family, particularly his two daughters. The warm relationship we see with them early in the novel prevents us from judging Hanne before we know her fully, and before she fully knows herself. Schuyler structures the novel so that Hanne's transformation does not occur in a simplistic, linear chronology; rather we experience Hanne's self-realization as Hanne experiences it—through memory and reflection.

The opportunity for such reflection arrives when Hanne suffers a fall. Out for a walk, having finished the translation, and begun work on a play she wants to write about a 10th-century female Japanese poet, Ono no Komachi, Hanne sees the golden dome of San Francisco City Hall, where she married her husband, a Japanese man she met when they were both graduate students at Columbia. When they separated, her problems with Brigitte increased and then intensified when he died suddenly of a heart attack. As she reminisces, we see a young playful Hanne, searching for the daily haiku her husband writes to her when they are dating. She uses the occasion of these happy memories to reassure herself that "Brigitte was wrong when she accused [her] of not loving him, of not loving anyone." Feeling sentimental, she wanders around in City Hall and is caught up in a crowd. She loses her footing and falls. Fading into a kind of hallucinatory unconsciousness, one of the lines from Kobayashi's novel that she struggled to translate appears before her: *"What you once loved lies there, inert, sucked of all its juices because you forgot it."*

When she regains consciousness in the hospital, she can only speak Japanese. While this has a neurological explanation, its immediate effect is that she can communicate with very few people. Tomas, unlike Brigitte, who (like her mother) was a wunderkind with languages but did not learn Japanese, struggled to learn the language and knows it well enough to speak with his mother and act as her translator as well when he visits her in the hospital and remains in touch with her throughout her recovery.

Though Hanne had earlier refused the Japanese Ministry of Culture's invitation to speak about her theory and practice of translation at a conference in Tokyo, she changes her mind when she is released from the hospital and can't talk to many people. She calls to see if Kobayashi is attending the conference, chatting at great length with the Japanese organizer of the conference after days of living in silence. When that is confirmed, she makes arrangements to leave for Tokyo, imagining that he will "request her to translate his next book" because "when a writer finds a translator who understands his work, it's like finding gold."

Much to her horror and humiliation, however, Kobayashi does not treat her like treasure; rather he interrupts her presentation with his noisy entrance and continual muttering. When she is finished, he accosts her, saying that what she believes is "idiotic. This idea that translation is purer than what the author creates." Furthermore he tells her, "You were supposed to translate my words, my story, not rewrite it and make your own story in the hopes of uniting mankind. I don't know where you get your ideas about translation, but no author in his right mind would want you to translate his work." In continuing to tell her how she ruined his main character, Jiro, Kobayashi mentions that Jiro is based on the famous Noh actor Moto Okuro, and adds that Moto would hate her translation.

Determined to prove that her Jiro is the true Jiro, she flees to the Japanese countryside where Moto lives, hoping to meet him and confirm that her translation is correct. Without some understanding of the depth of Hanne's trauma, this move would be almost unbelievable. Even the immature student of literature knows to take with a grain a salt the notion that works of art are *based on a true story*. But one of the things we have learned about Hanne via her memories is that she was a child trained to persevere.

Having followed her German parents, both translators, from one international post to the next, young Hanne found it difficult to make friends. When she returns from school one day in tears because classmates teased her, Hanne's mother told her, "You're a creature out of the ordinary, my dear," and that with "each new language [she] became, quite magically, larger and grander than before." Thus, she should neither expect to be understood, nor care when she isn't. "'*Halt die Ohren steif!*' Keep yours ears stiff!" her father told her. Along with a belief in the power of language, both parents impress upon young Hanne the necessity of staying strong and persevering at all costs. Should Hanne complain, she knows that her mother has at the ready the story of living with Hanne's Oma for two months in a basement apartment at the end of WWII, hiding from Soviet soldiers who "careen[ed] down the streets, stealing, destroying, raping. . . . We ate rats, so this hardship you speak of, it's nothing. A speck of dust."

In part because they have failure in common—Moto is unable to return to the stage and is a voice actor in commercials—Hanne and Moto develop a complicated relationship, one that will eventually crack the neurological code that revives her English. One night after drinking too much, Moto challenges Hanne to tell him something he doesn't know about her. In doing so, much to her surprise, Hanne reveals a secret: "I am used to being in many worlds at once. . . . Not the real world . . . but I found solace in the world of language. In my mind, I used to glide from one language to another to another."

While this might sound like an academic response, we have seen Hanne in the throes of deep humiliation when she learns that Kobayashi has pulled her translation of his novel and asked for a new one. She remembers a time when her mother, for reasons Hanne never understood, sent her to live with her cruel Oma whose mind had remained in the horror at the end of WWII. Oma forced Hanne to learn Russian so that they could negotiate with the soldiers Oma imagined coming to the door to rob or rape them. She made Hanne stand in the snow for hours if she spilt her milk and banished her to the cellar for wetting her bed.

> Once a rat crawled across her foot and she called out "Mama!" Oma called down to her that she'd have to stay another hour for making such a racket. So she put her back against the cold concrete wall and tried to will herself beyond the blackness by conjugating English verbs. *Scream, screamed, had screamed, screaming.*

It is in her often contentious relationship with Moto that Hanne becomes more empathetic, learns to experience her emotions without having to mitigate them with words. She returns to San Francisco with "a deep, raw longing for Brigitte" and the recognition that she had committed "A deliberate misreading of her daughter to bolster her, not just once but many times to cultivate something bold and resolute, something hearty and robust so the blows of the world would not break her like a cheap knickknack." She accepts the truth in Tomas's accusation that she had denied Brigitte's suffering so that she "could justify sending her to boarding school and believe she'd be fine." And she understands that she has burdened him with the responsibility of parenting Brigitte to some extent.

The conclusion of the novel is so surprising and profound that to discuss it in any detail would rob the reader of a moving experience. Suffice it to say that Hanne will be challenged to enact what she has learned about herself in a situation requiring both physical and emotional strength as well as a tolerance for silence that she would have previously found unbearable.

In Hanne Schubert—an older woman, a mother, a grandmother, an intelligent scholar—Schuyler has created a fascinating, multifaceted character who takes the hard-earned opportunity to translate her life into its truest, most honest story.

Able MUSE

A REVIEW OF POETRY, PROSE & ART

After more than a decade of online publishing excellence, Able Muse began a bold new chapter with its print edition

We continue to bring you in print the usual masterful craft with poetry, fiction, essays, art & photography, and book reviews

Check out our 12+ years of online archives for work by

RACHEL HADAS • X.J. KENNEDY • TIMOTHY STEELE • MARK JARMAN • A.E. STALLINGS • DICK DAVIS • A.M. JUSTER • TIMOTHY MURPHY • DEBORAH WARREN • CHELSEA RATHBURN • RHINA P. ESPAILLAT • TURNER CASSITY • RICHARD MOORE • STEPHEN EDGAR • ANNIE FINCH • THAISA FRANK • NINA SCHUYLER • SOLITAIRE MILES • MISHA GORDIN • & SEVERAL OTHERS

SUBSCRIPTION

Able Muse - Print Edition - Subscriptions:

Able Muse is published semiannually.
Subscription rates for individuals: $24.00 per year; single and previous issues: $16.95 + $3 S&H.
International subscription rate: $33 per year; single and previous issues: $16.95 + $5 S&H.
(All rates in USD.)

Subscribe online with PayPal/credit card **www.ablemusepress.com**

Or send a check payable to *Able Muse Review*
Attn: Alex Pepple - Editor, Able Muse, 467 Saratoga Avenue #602, San Jose, CA 95129 USA

Able Muse - Summer 2013

Print Edition, No. 15

WITH POETRY • FICTION • ESSAYS • BOOK REVIEWS • ART & PHOTOGRAPHY

142 pages
ISBN 978-1-927409-21-3

FEATURED ARTIST
Clara Lieu
(Interviewed by Sharon Passmore)

FEATURED POET
Greg Williamson
(Interviewed by Stephen Kampa)

★★★★★

POETRY, FICTION, BOOK REVIEWS, INTERVIEWS & ESSAYS FROM DICK ALLEN FRED LONGWORTH CATHARINE SAVAGE BROSMAN ROBERT J. LEVY LEN KRISAK CALLIE SISKEL D.R. GOODMAN HALEY HACH TIMOTHY MURPHY RAY NAYLER ROBERT SCHULTZ ILYA LYASHEVSKY RYAN WILSON DAVID MASON PETER BYRNE DAVID CAPLAN STEPHEN KAMPA DEREK FURR N.S. THOMPSON AND OTHERS

ORDER NOW FROM ABLE MUSE PRESS AT: WWW.ABLEMUSEPRESS.COM
OR, ORDER FROM AMAZON.COM, BN.COM, . . . & OTHER ONLINE OR OFFLINE BOOKSTORES

www.AbleMusePress.com

Able Muse Anthology

978-0-9865338-0-8 • $16.95

Edited by Alexander Pepple • *Foreword by* Timothy Steele

PRAISE FOR THE *ABLE MUSE ANTHOLOGY*:

This book fills an important gap in understanding what is really happening in early twenty-first century American poetry. **–Dana Gioia**

You hold in your hands a remarkable anthology of poems, translations, an interview, essays, short stories and visual art. **–David Mason**

This extraordinarily rich collection of fiction, poetry, essays and art by so many gifted enablers of the Muse is both a present satisfaction and a promise of future performance. **–Charles Martin**

Neither unskilled, lethargic, nor distracted from their proper enterprise, the muses in the past decade have been singularly able, as this outstanding anthology from *Able Muse* demonstrates. **–Catharine Savage Brosman**

Here's a generous serving of the cream of *Able Muse*, including not only formal verse but nonmetrical work that also displays careful craft, memorable fiction (seven remarkable stories), striking artwork and photography, and incisive critical prose. **–X. J. Kennedy**

Mark Jarman, Rachel Hadas, Turner Cassity, Stephen Edgar, Timothy Steele, R. S. Gwynn, Rhina P. Espaillat, A. M. Juster, Geoffrey Brock, Annie Finch, X. J. Kennedy, Timothy Murphy, Jennifer Reeser, Beth Houston, Dick Davis, A. E. Stallings, Richard Moore, Chelsea Rathburn, David Stephenson, Julie Kane, Alan Sullivan, Kim Bridgford, Deborah Warren, Diane Thiel, Richard Wakefield, Rose Kelleher, Leslie Monsour, Lyn Lifshin, Amit Majmudar, Len Krisak, Marilyn L. Taylor, Dolores Hayden, Suzanne J. Doyle, Dennis Must, Thaisa Frank, Nina Schuyler, Misha Gordin, Solitaire Miles, and others.

from **Able Muse Press**

Order or, find more information at: **www.ablemusepress.com**

Or, order at: **Amazon.com, BN.com, . . .**

& other popular online & offline bookstores

House Music

Poems

by Ellen Kaufman

***NEW~ *from* Able Muse Press**

Finalist, 2012 Able Muse Book Award

HOUSE MUSIC
(with a Foreword by Jennifer Barber)

The first full-length collection from Ellen Kaufman

★★★★★

"Ellen Kaufman is a master of sight; her explorations encourage us to see the ordinary beauty in homely scenes."
— Willard Spiegelman

"[Ellen Kaufman's] language is taut and her aim unerring: her poems fly straight and true."
— Jennifer Barber (from the foreword)

"The intelligence behind Ellen Kaufman's wonderfully realized House Music is poised and observant, its reflections unfolding in sinuous sentences that are effortlessly elegant and deceptively plainspoken."
— John Koethe

"Ellen Kaufman's distinguished poems . . . are astonishing acts of balance, intelligence, precision, eloquence, vision, imagination, and grace."
— Vijay Seshadri

ISBN 978-1-927409-25-1 / 94 pages

ORDER NOW FROM ABLE MUSE PRESS AT: WWW.ABLEMUSEPRESS.COM
OR, ORDER FROM AMAZON.COM, BN.COM, . . . & OTHER ONLINE OR OFFLINE BOOKSTORES

www.AbleMusePress.com

Credo for the Checkout Line in Winter

Poems

by Maryann Corbett

*NEW~ *from* Able Muse Press

CREDO for the CHECKOUT LINE in WINTER

poems | Maryann Corbett

WITH A FOREWORD BY PETER CAMPION

Finalist, 2011 Able Muse Book Award

PRAISE FOR *CREDO . . .*
(with a Foreword by Peter Campion)

The second collection of original poetry from Maryann Corbett

★★★★★

"She is a newborn Robert Frost, with a wicked eye for contemporary life."
— Willis Barnstone

"[She] remains a poet of the first order, and her poems are cause for gratitude, and deep enjoyment."
— Peter Campion (from the foreword)

"A stunning collection, from one of America's most gifted contemporary poets."
— Marilyn L. Taylor

"Sharply visual, skillfully and cleverly crafted."
— Catharine Savage Brosman

"Corbett is one of the best-kept secrets of American poetry, and this is one of the best new collections I've read in years."
— Geoffrey Brock

ISBN 978-1-927409-14-5 / 102 pages

ORDER NOW FROM ABLE MUSE PRESS AT: WWW.ABLEMUSEPRESS.COM
OR, ORDER FROM AMAZON.COM, BN.COM, . . . & OTHER ONLINE OR OFFLINE BOOKSTORES

www.AbleMusePress.com

Pumpkin Chucking

Poems

by Stephen Scaer

***NEW~ *from* Able Muse Press**

Pumpkin Chucking

POEMS

Stephen Scaer

With a Foreword by A.M. Juster

Finalist, 2012 Able Muse Book Award

PRAISE FOR *PUMPKIN CHUCKING*
(with a Foreword by A.M. Juster)

The first full-length collection from Stephen Scaer

★★★★★

". . . the prevailing voice in this collection belongs to a hugely entertaining, middle-aged, middle-class Everyman writing about the everyday."
— Deborah Warren

"Stephen Scaer's Pumpkin Chucking *celebrates the New England landscape while still being universal . . . with wit in the winking way of Frost."*
— A.M. Juster (from the foreword)

". . . a tour of the expressive possibilities of all of English poetry"
— Richard Wakefield

"This is a wonderful and entertaining book of poetry."
— Robert Crawford

ISBN 978-1-927409-12-1 / 90 pages

ORDER NOW FROM ABLE MUSE PRESS AT: WWW.ABLEMUSEPRESS.COM
OR, ORDER FROM AMAZON.COM, BN.COM, . . . & OTHER ONLINE OR OFFLINE BOOKSTORES

www.AbleMusePress.com

The Dark Gnu and Other Poems

written & illustrated by Wendy Videlock

***NEW~ *from* Able Muse Press**

The Second Full-Length Collection of Poetry from Wendy Videlock

★★★★★

"Wendy Videlock's poems contain laughing pears, rhyming coyotes, and jaded wind. In reading this book, I found myself laughing and gasping in equal measures. And cursing, as well, because Videlock is so damn good and I'm so damn jealous of her talent. She is one of my very favorite poets."
— Sherman Alexie

"Reminiscent in some ways of Shel Silverstein's classic collections, Videlock's new book, The Dark Gnu and Other Poems, *supplements sly whimsy with mystery and a hint of tragedy. These poems remind readers "of all inconceivable ages" that not all problems have solutions and that some narratives end in mystery rather than in resolution.* The Dark Gnu *is enhanced by the author's illustrations that deepen the allure of the poems."*
— Jeremy Telman

ISBN 978-1-927409-09-1 / 96 pages (paperback)
ISBN 978-1-927409-13-8 / 94 pages (Deluxe Edition - hardcover)

ORDER NOW FROM ABLE MUSE PRESS AT: WWW.ABLEMUSEPRESS.COM
OR, ORDER FROM AMAZON.COM, BN.COM, . . . & OTHER ONLINE OR OFFLINE BOOKSTORES

www.AbleMusePress.com

Corporeality

Stories

by Hollis Seamon

~ *from* **Able Muse Press**

Shortlisted Book: 2014 YALSA's Alex Awards

"...Seamon offers enough thematic and narrative variation to keep each story in this collection fresh." — *Publishers Weekly*

★★★★★

"It's a feast of language that you won't soon forget."
— *Alan Davis*

"These stories have grace, wit, adventure, danger, humor, compassion, magic, and rage. Hollis Seamon casts full and dazzling light on those who are often overlooked—teenaged lovebirds in a hospice, flood victims before the flood, plagiarists, arsonists, old ladies, fat dogs. She brings them to life so tenderly and powerfully that they stay with you, long after the last page."
— *Nalini Jones*

"These stories make memorable the people you wonder about in passing."
— *Eugenia Kim*

"What a magical collection! Hollis Seamon's enchanting stories will make you marvel anew at the forever strange, blessed, and heartbreaking affliction we share as human beings on this earth."
— *Edward Schwarzschild*

ISBN 978-1-927409-03-9 / 204 pages

ORDER NOW FROM ABLE MUSE PRESS AT: WWW.ABLEMUSEPRESS.COM
OR, ORDER FROM AMAZON.COM, BN.COM, . . . & OTHER ONLINE OR OFFLINE BOOKSTORES

www.AbleMusePress.com

Heaven from Steam

Poems

by Carol Light

***NEW~ *from* Able Muse Press**

Finalist, 2012 Able Muse Book Award

PRAISE FOR *HEAVEN FROM STEAM*
(with a Foreword by Brad Leithauser)

The first full-length collection from Carol Light

★★★★★

"Carol Light's Heaven from Steam *is an extraordinary book, formally adept and wonderfully inventive. [It] is a thrilling debut."*
— Jason Whitmarsh

"The book is marked by a lightness of touch. The overall effect is playful."
— Brad Leithauser (from the foreword)

"Carol Light, in Heaven from Steam, performs arias again and again; her songs are equal parts rapturous . . . and disquieting"
— Cody Walker

"Although these poems span landscapes from the Pacific Northwest to Italy, their true settings are interior, the complex terrain of an acutely observant and questioning mind."
— Linda Bierds

ISBN 978-1-927409-18-3 / 108 pages

ORDER NOW FROM ABLE MUSE PRESS AT: WWW.ABLEMUSEPRESS.COM
OR, ORDER FROM AMAZON.COM, BN.COM, . . . & OTHER ONLINE OR OFFLINE BOOKSTORES

www.AbleMusePress.com

Compositions of the Dead Playing Flutes

Poems

by Barbara Ellen Sorensen

***NEW~ *from* Able Muse Press**

PRAISE FOR *COMPOSITIONS OF THE DEAD PLAYING FLUTES*
(with a Foreword by Veronica Patterson)

The first full-length collection from Barbara Ellen Sorensen

★★★★★

"Barbara Ellen Sorensen's Compositions of the Dead Playing Flutes *is a book of stunning wakefulness. For it is a wake, but at the same time a celebration, one that focuses on places where the dead were once most alive, places where we are most acutely seen and heard."*
— Matthew Cooperman

"These poems are attentive, scrupulous, and transforming, as they range from the sensuous to the spiritual."
— Veronica Patterson (from the foreword)

"Barbara Ellen Sorensen is . . . a modern Ovid offering metamorphoses of the triumphs and ashes of human existence in a voice at once deeply personal and entirely of us all."
— Suzanne Paola

ISBN 978-1-927409-23-7 / 132 pages

ORDER NOW FROM ABLE MUSE PRESS AT: WWW.ABLEMUSEPRESS.COM
OR, ORDER FROM AMAZON.COM, BN.COM, . . . & OTHER ONLINE OR OFFLINE BOOKSTORES

www.AbleMusePress.com

Strange Borderlands

Poems

by Ben Berman

*NEW~ *from* **Able Muse Press**

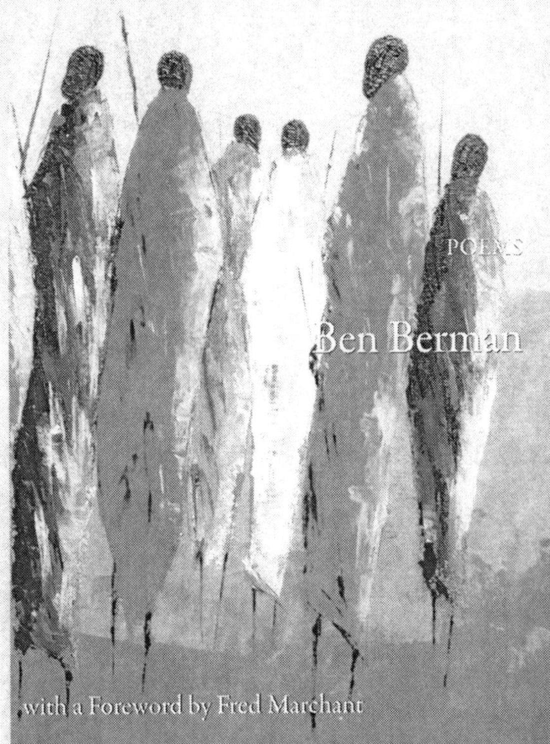

PRAISE FOR *STRANGE BORDERLANDS*
(with a Foreword by Fred Marchant)

★★★★★

"Ben Berman's debut poetry collection is a compelling examination of the author's experiences in Zimbabwe as a Peace Corps volunteer. . . . This is a must-have book for readers of poetry." — *Publishers Weekly,* Starred Review

"Ben Berman's lyric poems set in Zimbabwe dig deep into the casual and the casualty of daily life . . . I believe every word in this collection. This is an unforgettable debut by a powerful and humble voice."
— Dzvinia Orlowsky

"These are poems that weigh, consider, and restore some flesh-and-blood meaning to the experience of multiculturalism, a word so overused it is often flattened out to a platitude or piety. But not in this book."
— Fred Marchant (from the "Foreword")

"What's most impressive about this terrific book is Berman's inclusive generous spirit, the deadly serious imaginative play he exercises in every line of every poem. This is a book to cherish."
— Alan Shapiro

ISBN 978-1-927409-03-9 / 104 pages

ORDER NOW FROM ABLE MUSE PRESS AT: WWW.ABLEMUSEPRESS.COM
OR, ORDER FROM AMAZON.COM, BN.COM, . . . & OTHER ONLINE OR OFFLINE BOOKSTORES

www.AbleMusePress.com

~ *from* **Able Muse Press**

This Bed Our Bodies Shaped
Poems
by April Lindner

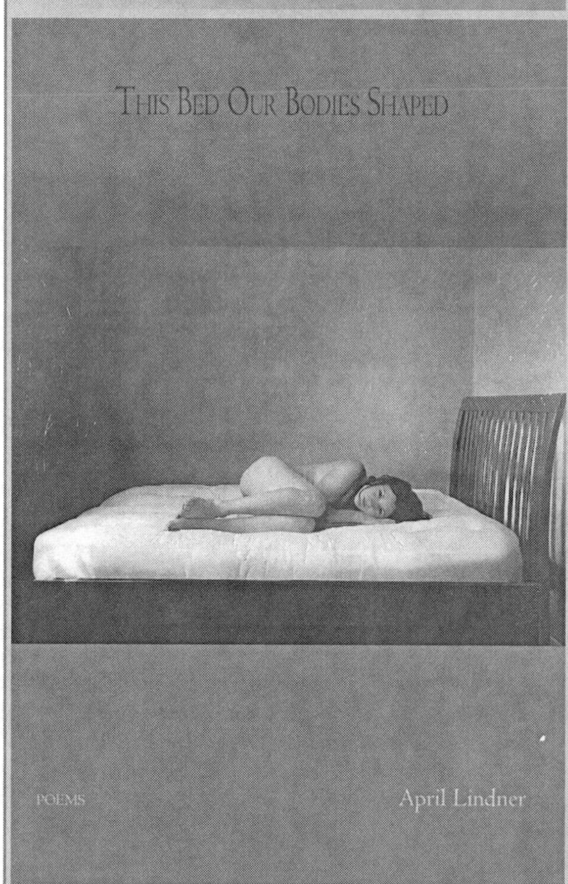

"All the pleasures and pains of domestic life, of marriage and parenthood, love and loss, dailiness and major rites of passage, find their textures and music in the poems of April Lindner's new collection."
— Mark Jarman

Life in the Second Circle
Poems
by Michael Cantor

"Like Muhammad Ali, one of the "Box Men" he celebrates in a virtuosic crown of sonnets, Cantor is a master of floating like a butterfly in a small, roped-off space."
— Catherine Tufariello

www.AbleMusePress.com

~ *from* **Able Muse Press**

The Cosmic Purr

Poems

by Aaron Poochigian

A Vertical Mile

Poems

by Richard Wakefield

The Cosmic Purr

POEMS

Aaron Poochigian

With a Foreword by Charles Martin

A VERTICAL MILE

Richard Wakefield

POEMS

With a Foreword by David Sanders

"A major translator from classical Greek, Poochigian offers in his own poetry a hip formality, a timeless sense of the contemporary."
— David Mason

"As a poet of the outdoors—one who sees and, seeing, makes new what he has seen—Wakefield is unsurpassed."
— R.S. Gwynn

www.AbleMusePress.com

Grasshopper:
The Poetry of M A Griffiths

~ *Now reprinted & distributed in the USA & Canada by* **Able Muse Press**

Grasshopper

The Poetry of

M A Griffiths

Margaret Ann Griffiths (1947-2009)

Margaret was born and raised in London and lived for some time in Bracknell then later moved to Poole. Rather than seek publication through traditional channels, she was content to share her work with fellow poets on various Internet forums. On the rare occasions she submitted work for publication, it was typically to online venues. Also known by the Internet pseudonyms "Grasshopper" and "Maz," she began posting her poetry online in 2001. During the mid-2000s she worked from home, running a small Internet-based business, and edited the *Poetry Worm*, a monthly periodical distributed by email.

In 2008, her "Opening a Jar of Dead Sea Mud" won *Eratosphere*'s annual Sonnet Bake-off, and was praised by Richard Wilbur. Later that year she was a Guest Poet on the Academy of American Poets website, where she was hailed as "one of the up-and-coming poets of our time."

She suffered for years from a stomach ailment which eventually proved fatal in July 2009. Almost immediately after her death was announced on *Eratosphere*, poets from all over the English-speaking world, from London, Derby, Scotland, Wales, Queensland, New South Wales, Massachusetts, New York, Minnesota, Missouri, Maryland, California and Texas collected her work for this publication.

- First published by Arrowhead Press in the UK (January, 2011)
- Reprinted and distributed in the USA and Canada by Able Muse Press (April, 2011)

ISBN 978-1-904852-28-5 / 384 pages

ORDER NOW FROM ABLE MUSE PRESS AT: WWW.ABLEMUSEPRESS.COM

OR, ORDER FROM AMAZON.COM, BN.COM, . . . & OTHER ONLINE OR OFFLINE BOOKSTORES

www.AbleMusePress.com

~ *from* **Able Muse Press**

Lines of Flight

Poems

by Catherine Chandler

"... an authoritative new voice. Chandler writes with drive and force, and yet is able to convey what she calls 'the delicate forensics of the heart.'"
— X.J. Kennedy

Nevertheless

Poems

by Wendy Videlock

Nevertheless

COLORADO BOOK AWARDS

21st

1991 · ANNUAL · 2012

POEMS

Wendy Videlock

FINALIST, 2012
COLORADO BOOK AWARDS

With a Foreword by A.E. Stallings

"Videlock is a magician of play and pleasures, wisdom being not the least of these."
— A.E. Stallings

www.AbleMusePress.com

Dirge for an Imaginary World

Poems

by Matthew Buckley Smith

~ *from* **Able Muse Press**

WINNER
2011 Able Muse Book Award

PRAISE FOR *DIRGE FOR AN IMAGINARY WORLD*
(with a Foreword by Greg Williamson)

The first full-length collection from Matthew Buckley Smith

★★★★★

"The comic is rich with serious intent and gravity lightened with discerning wit."
— Andrew Hudgins (Judge, 2011 Able Muse Book Award)

"Mental and linguistic agility generously challenge the reader in poem after poem."
— Greg Williamson (from the "Foreword")

"These are poems full of both reckoning and grace, made all the more beautiful for their humane wisdom."
— Carrie Jerrell

ISBN 978-0-9878705-0-6 / 80 pages
ORDER NOW FROM **ABLE MUSE PRESS** AT: WWW.ABLEMUSEPRESS.COM
OR, ORDER FROM **AMAZON.COM, BN.COM**, . . . & OTHER ONLINE OR OFFLINE BOOKSTORES

www.AbleMusePress.com

CONTRIBUTOR NOTES

MELISSA BALMAIN's poetry collection, *Walking in on People,* was chosen by X.J. Kennedy as the winner of the 2013 Able Muse Book Award and will be published in 2014 by Able Muse Press. She is the editor of *Light,* an online journal of light verse (formerly *Light Quarterly*). She teaches at the University of Rochester.

RACHAEL BRIGGS, when she's not writing poetry, works as a research fellow in philosophy. She splits her time between Griffith University in Brisbane, Queensland, Australia, and the Australian National University in Canberra, ACT, Australia. She has published poems in *Rattle* and *The Tower Journal,* and likes to perform at a variety of Brisbane venues, including Words or Whatever, Speedpoets, Riverbend Poets, Whispers Salon and the Queensland Poetry Festival. Her first collection of poems, *Free Logic,* was published with the University of Queensland Press in 2013.

CATHARINE SAVAGE BROSMAN, PhD, is Professor Emerita of French at Tulane University. She was Mellon Professor of Humanities for 1990 and later held the Gore Chair in French. She was also visiting professor for a term at the University of Sheffield, UK. Her scholarly publications comprise eighteen books on French literary history and criticism. A new volume, *Louisiana Creole Literature: A Historical Study,* has just been published. She has published two collections of personal essays and nine collections of verse, including *Under the Pergola* (2011) and *On the North Slope* (2012). Her tenth collection, *On the Old Plaza,* is in press. New poems and essays are out or forthcoming in *The South Carolina Review, Sewanee Review, Méasŭre, Modern Age,* and *Southwest Review.*

PETER BYRNE partakes of the lyric opera that is Italian life from Lecce, his home at the southern tip of the peninsula. The idyllic location, not that far from the Vatican and the historic birthplace of the Mafia, hasn't escaped the nervousness now traversing the European Union. But in the face of "austerity" Peter still "worships language and forgives."

CHRIS CHILDERS teaches at St. Andrew's School in Middletown, Delaware. He is hard at work translating a volume of Greek and Latin lyric poetry for Penguin Classics.

JEHANNE DUBROW—SEE page 101.

Anna M. Evans's poems have appeared or are forthcoming in the *Harvard Review, Atlanta Review, Rattle, American Arts Quarterly,* and *32 Poems.* She gained her MFA from Bennington College, and is the editor of the *Raintown Review.* Recipient of Fellowships from the MacDowell Artists' Colony and the Virginia Center for the Creative Arts, and winner of the 2012 Rattle Poetry Prize Readers' Choice Award, she currently teaches at West Windsor Art Center and Richard Stockton College of NJ. Her fifth chapbook, *Selected Poems of Marceline Desbordes-Valmore,* is forthcoming from Barefoot Muse Press.

D.R. Goodman, a native of Oak Ridge, Tennessee, studied biology at Reed College in Oregon and philosophy at UC Berkeley, before leaving academia to practice writing and martial arts. She lives in Oakland, California, where she is founder and chief instructor at a martial arts school. Her poetry has appeared in such journals as *Crazyhorse, Notre Dame Review, Seattle Review, Tampa Review, Whitefish Review,* and many others; and in the 2005 anthology, *Sonnets: 150 Contemporary Sonnets,* William Baer, editor. She is also the author of *The Kids' Karate Workbook: A Take-Home Training Guide for Young Martial Artists,* from North Atlantic/Blue Snake Books; and of an illustrated chapbook, *Birds by the Bay.*

Alex Greenberg is a 14-year-old aspiring poet. His work can be found or is forthcoming in *The Louisville Review, The Literary Bohemian, Cuckoo Quarterly, My Favorite Bullet, The Boiler, Burningword Literary Journal, Spinning Jenny, Cadaverine,* and *Literary Juice.* He was the runner-up in Challenges 1 and 2 of the Cape Farewell SWITCH Poetry Competition. He has won a gold key in the Scholastic Arts and Writings Awards and was named a Foyle Young Poet of 2012 and 2013.

R.S. (Sam) Gwynn has taught at Lamar University, in Beaumont, Texas, since 1976. Many of his former students are publishing poets.

Rachel Hadas is Board of Governors Professor of English at the Newark campus of Rutgers University, where she has taught for many years. The most recent of her many books are a collection of poetry, *The Golden Road* (Northwestern University Press, 2012), and a memoir, *Strange Relation* (Paul Dry Books, 2011).

Jane Hammons teaches writing at UC Berkeley. Her writing appears in several anthologies including *Hint Fiction: An Anthology of Stories in 25 Words or Fewer* (W.W. Norton); *The Maternal is Political* (Seal Press); and *California Prose Directory: New Writing from the Golden State* (Outpost 19). A collection of short stories was recently short listed for The Scott Prize by Salt Publishing. She has published fiction and nonfiction in a variety of magazines and journals, such as *Alaska Quarterly Review, Columbia Journalism Review, San Francisco Chronicle Magazine, Southwestern American Literature* and *Word Riot.* For *Bloom,* she writes about writers whose first significant work was published after age 40.

STEPHEN HARVEY serves as assistant professor of Anesthesiology at Vanderbilt University Medical Center. He has published poems in *Able Muse, Linebreak,* the *Literary Bohemian,* and in medical literature. He was inspired to write "Last Dance" when his one-year-old daughter played with a friend's father, William Dennis Helsabeck, Sr. Dr. Helsabeck died in January 2013, at the age of 100.

ELISE HEMPEL lives in central Illinois. Her poems have appeared in many journals over the years, including *Méasüre, Valparaiso Poetry Review, Spoon River Poetry Review,* and *Borderlands: Texas Poetry Review.*

CHERYL DIANE KIDDER has a BA in creative writing from San Francisco State University. Her work, nominated twice for the Pushcart Prize, has appeared or is forthcoming in: *CutThroat Magazine, Weber—The Contemporary West, Pembroke Magazine, Able Muse, decomP Magazine, Tinge Magazine, Brevity Magazine, Brain,Child Magazine, Identity Theory, In Posse Review,* and elsewhere.

DONNA LAEMMLEN's stories appear in *Tin House* online, *Fourteen Hills, SmokeLong Quarterly, Slice Magazine, Switchback Literary Journal,* the anthology *Flash 101: Surviving the Fiction Apocalypse,* and elsewhere. Her flash fiction "Centerville" was recently performed at *Stories on Stage.* She earned her MFA from the University of San Francisco, and is an award-winning screenwriter who teaches graduate and undergraduate film studies at the Academy of Art University.

AMANDA LUECKING FROST recently completed her PhD in English and Creative Writing at the University of Kansas. She was a Michener Fellow at the University of Texas at Austin where she received her MFA. She received her BA from the University of Michigan, Ann Arbor. She is nonfiction editor of the current issue of *Beecher's Magazine* (no. 3) and was associate editor of *Bat City Review.* Her most recent work appears in *Blue Island Review* and *Coal City Review.*

CHRISSY MASON hails from the island of Tasmania, famous for apples and wilderness. She moved, for love, to the United States in 2012. She lives many lives. The life she loves is always on the move.

DAVID MASON lives and writes and travels with his wife, Chrissy. Two new books will appear in 2014: *Sea Salt: Poems of a Decade* and *Davey McGravy: Tales for Children and Adult Children.* He is Poet Laureate of Colorado, and also has a home in Oregon.

PHILIP MORRE lives and works as a translator in Venice, Italy. His most recent book of poetry is *The Sadness of Animals* (San Marco Press, 2012).

JOHN SAVOIE teaches great books at Southern Illinois University, Edwardsville. His poems have appeared in *Poetry* and *Best New Poets,* and his first collection, *Open Book, Empty Cup,* is ready for a publisher.

MATTHEW BUCKLEY SMITH was the winner of the 2011 Able Muse Book Award for his first collection, *Dirge for an Imaginary World*. His poems have been nominated for Pushcart Prizes and featured in *32 Poems, Beloit Poetry Journal, Commonweal,* and *Iron Horse Literary Review,* as well as in *Verse Daily* and *Best American Poetry*. His reviews have appeared in *32 Poems Blog, Innisfree Poetry Journal, The Journal, Méasŭre,* and *Verse.* His plays have been performed in Baltimore, London, and Washington, DC. He lives in Baltimore with his wife, Joanna Pearson.

A.E. STALLINGS is an American poet who studied Classics in Athens, Georgia, and has lived in Athens, Greece, since 1999. She has published a verse translation of Lucretius for Penguin Classics, *The Nature of Things.* Her most recent collection of poems is *Olives.*

PETER SVENSSON—SEE page 69.

TARA TATUM is 26 years old and grew up in Southeast Texas, where she received her MA in English at Lamar University. She is currently working on her MFA in poetry at the University of Florida.

BLAINE VITALLO is a middle-school tutor and full-time college student studying English and education at the University of Florida. A Florida native who's also lived in Illinois, he's been writing for about three years but has never been published until now.

JEANNE WAGNER is the recipient of several national awards, including 2012 Saranac Review Prize and the 2012 Thomas Merton Poetry of the Sacred Award. Her poems have appeared in *Southern Poetry Review, RHINO, Cincinnati Review, Alaska Quarterly Review,* and Ted Kooser's *American Life in Poetry.* She is on the editorial board of *California Quarterly.* She has five collections of poetry; the most recent, *In the Body of Our Lives,* was released by Sixteen Rivers press in 2011.

RICHARD WAKEFIELD's first collection of poetry, *East of Early Winters,* won the Richard Wilbur Award for 2006. His sonnet "Petrarch" won the 2010 Howard Nemerov Sonnet Award. His latest poetry collection, *A Vertical Mile,* was published by Able Muse Press in 2013. He teaches American literature and composition at a college in Tacoma, Washington, and for almost thirty years has been a literary critic for the *Seattle Times.*

RORY WATERMAN's first collection, *Tonight the Summer's Over,* a Poetry Book Society Recommendation, was published by Carcanet in November 2013. He works at Nottingham Trent University, coedits *New Walk,* and writes regularly for the *TLS* and other publications.

CHARLES WILKINSON's publications include *The Snowman and Other Poems* (Iron Press, 1987), *The Pain Tree and Other Stories* (London Magazine Editions, 2000) and *Ag & Au* (Flarestack Poets, 2013). His short stories have appeared in anthologies published by Heinemann, Unthank Books, Minerva and Little, Brown in the UK and in *Best English Short Stories II* (Norton, USA). He lives in Powys, Wales, where he is heavily outnumbered by members of the ovine community.

James Matthew Wilson is the author of *Four Verse Letters, Timothy Steele: A Critical Introduction,* and *The Violent and the Fallen* (Finishing Line Press, 2013). An award-winning scholar of philosophical-theology and literature, he teaches at Villanova University and lives in the village of Berwyn, Pennsylvania, with his wife and children.

Marly Youmans is the author of four books of poetry and seven of fiction, including five novels and two Southern fantasies for young adults. In the past year, she served on the National Book Award-YPL judging panel and published three books in three countries: a collection of formal poems, *The Foliate Head* (Stanza Press, UK), now in second printing; a long adventure in blank verse, *Thaliad* (Phoenicia Publishing, Montreal); and a novel from Mercer University Press, *A Death at the White Camellia Orphanage* (winner of The Ferrol Sams Award and the silver award for fiction in the ForeWord Book of the Year Awards). Both recent poetry books are strikingly decorated by artist Clive Hicks-Jenkins of Wales.

Able Muse - Winter 2012

Print Edition, No. 14

WITH THE 2012 ABLE MUSE WRITE PRIZE FOR POETRY & FICTION

212 pages
ISBN 978-1-927409-07-7

Includes the winning story and poems from the 2012 contest winners and finalists.

FEATURED ARTIST
Nicolas Evariste

FEATURED POET
Catherine Tufariello
(Interviewed by Uche Ogbuji)

★★★★★

POETRY, FICTION, BOOK REVIEWS, INTERVIEWS & ESSAYS FROM CATHARINE SAVAGE BROSMAN THOMAS CARPER LORNA KNOWLES BLAKE RICHARD WAKEFIELD TIMOTHY MURPHY KATHRYN LOCEY TONY BARNSTONE LEN KRISAK LEWIS BUZBEE EVELYN SOMERS GIGI MARK GREGORY DOWLING MICHAEL COHEN PETER BYRNE AARON POOCHIGIAN AND OTHERS

ORDER NOW FROM ABLE MUSE PRESS AT: WWW.ABLEMUSEPRESS.COM
OR, ORDER FROM AMAZON.COM, BN.COM, . . . & OTHER ONLINE OR OFFLINE BOOKSTORES

www.AbleMusePress.com

Able Muse - Inaugural Print Edition

Winter 2010

With

poetry, fiction, book reviews, interviews & essays from massimo sbreni ▪ r.p. lister ▪ catherine tufariello ▪ catharine savage brosman ▪ leslie monsour ▪ ned balbo ▪ susan mclean ▪ j. patrick lewis ▪ gail white ▪ kim bridgford ▪ nancy lou canyon ▪ john whitworth ▪ peter filkins ▪ marilyn l. taylor ▪ and others

ISBN 978-0-9865338-2-2

~ GET YOUR COPY AT ~

Able Muse Press: www.ablemusepress.com

Or

Amazon Worldwide: www.amazon.com

Able MUSE

A REVIEW OF POETRY, PROSE & ART

After more than a decade of online publishing excellence, Able Muse began a bold new chapter with its print edition

Check out our 12+ years of online archives for work by

Rachel Hadas • X.J. Kennedy • Timothy Steele • Mark Jarman • A.E. Stallings • Dick Davis • A.M. Juster • Timothy Murphy • Annie Finch • Deborah Warren • Chelsea Rathburn • Rhina P. Espaillat • Turner Cassity • Richard Moore • Stephen Edgar • David Mason • Thaisa Frank • • Nina Schuyler • Solitaire Miles • Misha Gordin • and others

SUBSCRIPTION

Able Muse - Print Edition

Able Muse is published semiannually.
Subscription rates for individuals: $24.00 per year;
single and previous issues: $16.95 + $3 S&H.

International subscription rate: $33 per year;
single and previous issues: $16.95 + $5 S&H.
(USD throughout.)

Subscribe online with PayPal/ credit card at

www.ablemusepress.com

Or send a check payable to *Able Muse Review*

Attn: Alex Pepple - Editor, Able Muse,
467 Saratoga Avenue #602,
San Jose, CA 95129 USA

Sailing to Babylon

Poems

by James Pollock

***NEW~ *from* Able Muse Press**

Finalist, 2012, Governor General Literary Awards (Canada)

Shortlisted Book, 2013: The Griffin Poetry Prize

PRAISE FOR *SAILING TO BABYLON* (*with a Foreword by Jeffery Donaldson*)

★★★★★

"Quietly confident, formally adept, assured in their music, these artful lyrics are not only an accomplishment in themselves but promise to register, as the poet says, 'the breaking changes of a life to come'."
— *Mark Doty, Judge's Citation, Griffin Poetry Prize shortlist*

"... A rich and complex array of subjects and allusions to provide both pleasure and challenge."
—Pleiades: A Journal of New Writing

"In Pollock's unadorned style, forged as it is in traditional forms . . . we get a vision of an old world, freighted with history, and still able to astonish itself with the novelty of its recurrence."
— *Michael Lista,* The National Post

ISBN 978-0-9865338-7-7 / 80 pages

ORDER NOW FROM ABLE MUSE PRESS AT: WWW.ABLEMUSEPRESS.COM
OR, ORDER FROM AMAZON.COM, BN.COM, . . . & OTHER ONLINE OR OFFLINE BOOKSTORES

www.AbleMusePress.com

INDEX

Symbols

A

B

C

D

E

P

R

S

T

U

V

W

Y

Able Muse - Summer 2012

Print Edition, No. 13

WITH THE 2011 ABLE MUSE WRITE PRIZE FOR POETRY HONORABLE MENTIONS

190 pages
ISBN 978-1-927409-01-5

FEATURED ARTIST
Andrew Ponomarenko

FEATURED POET
Patricia Smith
(Interviewed by Reginald Dwayne Betts)

★★★★★

POETRY, FICTION, BOOK REVIEWS, INTERVIEWS & ESSAYS FROM WENDY VIDELOCK CATHARINE SAVAGE BROSMAN TIMOTHY MURPHY JENNIFER REESER RICHARD WAKEFIELD JULIE BRUCK M.A. SCHAFFNER NED BALBO JAY ROGOFF ANNA M. EVANS KIM BRIDGFORD GALE ACUFF BRIAN CULHANE REGINALD DWAYNE BETTS MICHAEL GEORGE BRUCE BROMLEY AND OTHERS

ORDER NOW FROM ABLE MUSE PRESS AT: WWW.ABLEMUSEPRESS.COM
OR, ORDER FROM AMAZON.COM, BN.COM, . . . & OTHER ONLINE OR OFFLINE BOOKSTORES

www.AbleMusePress.com

Able Muse - Winter 2011

Print Edition, No. 12

WITH THE 2011 ABLE MUSE WRITE PRIZE FOR POETRY & FICTION

230 pages
ISBN 978-0-9865338-9-1

Includes the winning story and poems from the contest winners and finalists.

FEATURED ARTIST — Alper Çukur; (Interviewed by Sharon Passmore)

FEATURED POET — David Mason (Interviewed by David J. Rothman)

★★★★★

POETRY, FICTION, BOOK REVIEWS, INTERVIEWS & ESSAYS FROM SUZANNE J. DOYLE CATHARINE SAVAGE BROSMAN TIMOTHY MURPHY GABRIEL SPERA RICHARD WAKEFIELD SUSAN MCLEAN LYN LIFSHIN GEORGE WITTE AMIT MAJMUDAR JEAN L. KREILING RACHEL BENTLEY DOUGLAS CAMPBELL ANDREW FRISARDI DAVID J. ROTHMAN MICHAEL COHEN AND OTHERS

ORDER NOW FROM ABLE MUSE PRESS AT: WWW.ABLEMUSEPRESS.COM
OR, ORDER FROM AMAZON.COM, BN.COM, . . . & OTHER ONLINE OR OFFLINE BOOKSTORES

www.AbleMusePress.com

CPSIA information can be obtained at www.ICGtesting.com
Printed in the USA
BVOW08s2225151213

338663BV00011B/33/P